WARM MODERNITY

Warm Modernity

Indian Architecture Building Democracy

MADDALENA D'ALFONSO

SilvanaEditoriale

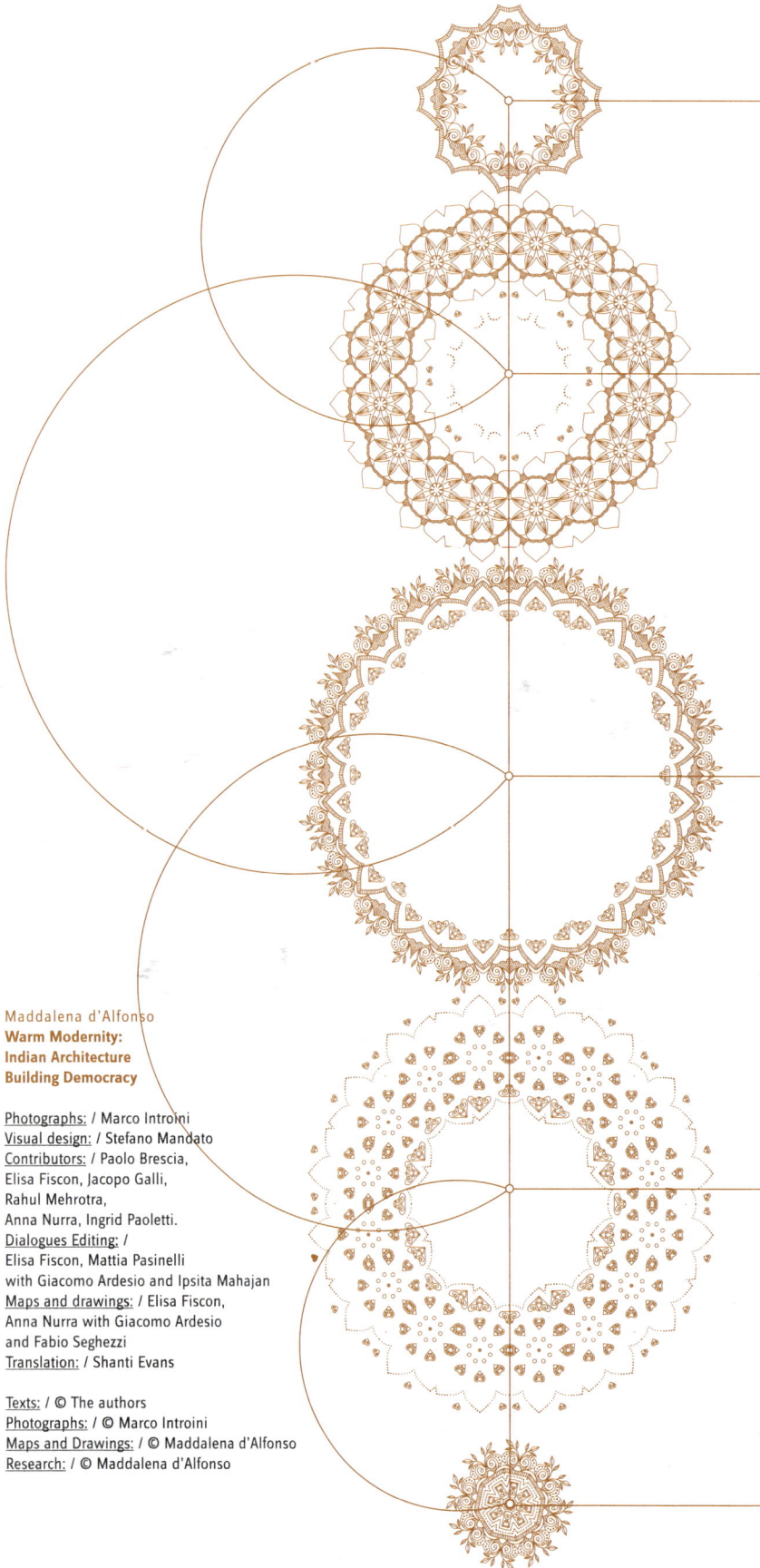

a

INTRO-
DUCTION

b

IMPORTING
MODERNITY

c

MODERNITY
AS A TOOL

d

EXPORTING
MODERNITY

e

BIBLIO-
GRAPHY

Maddalena d'Alfonso
**Warm Modernity:
Indian Architecture
Building Democracy**

Photographs: / Marco Introini
Visual design: / Stefano Mandato
Contributors: / Paolo Brescia,
Elisa Fiscon, Jacopo Galli,
Rahul Mehrotra,
Anna Nurra, Ingrid Paoletti.
Dialogues Editing: /
Elisa Fiscon, Mattia Pasinelli
with Giacomo Ardesio and Ipsita Mahajan
Maps and drawings: / Elisa Fiscon,
Anna Nurra with Giacomo Ardesio
and Fabio Seghezzi
Translation: / Shanti Evans

Index of contents

Storytelling ^{Maddalena d'Alfonso} / 6 /

Tropical Costants ^{Maps} / 10 /

Architects of interest ^{Timelines} / 20 /

The Indian Paradigm: The Definition of the Modern Tropical Landscape ^{Maddalena d'Alfonso} / 27 /

Establishing an Architectural Identity in an Age of Globalization ^{Paolo Brescia} / 38 /

Urban Tropical Landscape ^{Photographs by Marco Introini} / 42 /

Interpretative filters / 78 /

An Industrial City JAMSHEDPUR ^{Maddalena d'Alfonso} / 80 /

Modern Times ^{Anna Nurra} / 82 /

DIALOGUE WITH Balkrishna V. Doshi / 92 /

A Capital City BHUBANESWAR ^{Maddalena d'Alfonso} / 98 /

Urban Mandala ^{Elisa Fiscon} / 100 /

DIALOGUE WITH A.G. Krishna Menon / 110 /

A Town for Refugees FARIDABAD ^{Maddalena d'Alfonso} / 116 /

Players and Playgrounds ^{Maddalena d'Alfonso} / 118 /

Redrawing Chandigarh ^{Photographs by Marco Introini} / 130 /

What are we talking about when we speak about Participatory Architecture? ^{Maddalena d'Alfonso} / 164 /

A Further Dialogue ^{Maps} / 174 /

Tools of Participation. The Role of Design Manuals in Colonial and Postcolonial History ^{Jacopo Galli} / 184 /

Indigenous Technologies and Self-construction ^{Ingrid Paoletti} / 188 /

Architects in the Tropics ^{Maps + Timelines} / 192 /

DIALOGUE WITH Rahul Mehrotra / 200 /

INTRO–
DUCTION

STORYTELLING

/

MADDALENA D'ALFONSO

THIS BOOK IS A JOURNEY that I hope will keep your interest for a few moments. And that you will let yourself be carried beyond the history of the places of which it speaks into more contemporary territory.

The research commenced with my first visit to India in 2009. The first stop was to be Ahmedabad—where we would go to see the architecture of Le Corbusier, Louis Kahn and Balkrishna Doshi—and the last Chandigarh—the city of the modern myth. Purely by chance I paid a visit to Gandhinagar and, seeing the way it was clearly derived from Chandigarh, began to ask myself questions. Despite being on vacation, I couldn't resist giving in to my curiosity and the temptation to do some rummaging in the library of the Department of Architecture at CEPT University, another notable modern building. In a library that was incredibly dusty but highly efficient I discovered Otto Koenigsberger and the key role he played in the development of modern architecture and city planning in India. I would like to thank all the people who have been helping me up to now to satisfy my instinctive interest.

Five years have passed since that occasion and events linked to my research work have followed one another in a fortuitous and surreal manner, and one that was often discouraging and depressing. Surprisingly, however, the whole thing has turned out every day to be more and more closely linked to the living history of the present.

The publication, therefore, is the fruit of different moments of research, each structured and conceived to deal with materials of a different nature.
The first involved the preparation for and carrying out of a small survey of newly founded Indian towns and cities. Completed in August 2010, it led to the publica-

tion of an article in the invaluable Spanish magazine *Lars: cultura y ciudad*, whose editor at the time was Carlos Perez. The aim of this direct observation was to allow me to look for confirmation of my ideas and for archive materials.

Later came the supervision of two graduate theses, whose main objective was a redrawing of the architectural and urban models adopted in the new towns protocol. This first study made it possible to understand the paradigm of the band town pattern. The theses were those of Michele Vianello at the IUAV, "Gandhinagar territorio di una nuova modernità extraeuropea" ["Gandhinagar: Territory of a New Non-European Modernity"], and of Anna Nurra at Milan Polytechnic, "L'urbanistica tropicale di Otto Königsberger" ["Otto Königsberger's Tropical City Planning"].

A third moment sprang from the possibility of India having a pavilion at the 14th Venice Biennale of Architecture in 2014. When the theme Absorbing Modernity proposed by Rem Koolhaas for the national pavilions was announced I decided to send him an abstract of the research. To my surprise he liked it and suggested I curate the Indian Pavilion. We started doing all the necessary paperwork and, in parallel, set up an Italo-Indian research group that would be able to define the new insights and bring new lifeblood to the project.
Unfortunately political questions, quite outside the control of the people involved, made it impossible to carry it out. My thanks go to the Indian Embassy and the Venice Biennale for the efforts they made to keep it alive right until the end. I would also like to thank Paolo Brescia and Ingrid Paoletti, who have supplemented my studies and listened with interest to the new directions in which I wanted to go; without their support I would have been lost.
But above all my gratitude goes to Giacomo Ardesio—junior curator of the project for the pavilion—now at the OMA studio, whose energy made some dark moments simple and joyful to cope with.

The current research, finally, is the fruit of a decision taken with Rahul Mehrotra during the opening days of the 14th Venice Biennale of Architecture, entitled *Fundamentals*. In Venice it was clear to us that the absence of a reflection in depth on the sense of modernity in a country like India limits, in this day and age, understanding of the forms of design and planning and the devising of new paradigms that could be put into effect in the immediate future.
We agreed that I would bring the research to a conclusion by revealing its implications for the present day. I embarked on the final stage in the research with Elisa Fiscon's graduate thesis, "Bhubaneswar sfide di modernità in India" ["Bhubaneswar: Challenges of Modernity in India"].

The beginning of the end—i.e. the collection of the concluding materials—was a journey, not just to the cities presented as case studies (Jamshedpur, Bhubaneswar, Faridabad) but to Ahmedabad, Delhi, Mumbai and Agra as well. The expedition with Anna, Elisa and Giacomo was a regenerative and stimulating one. We interviewed Rahul Mehrotra, the architects who were directly involved in the definition of a specifically Indian language—Balkrishna V. Doshi, Raj Rewal, A.G. Krishna Menon—Bimal Patel, Ipsita Mahajan and the activists of URBZ—Matias Enchanove and Rahul Srivastava.
Their accounts and advice led us to discover the historical roots of Mughal architecture and prompted us to go to see the urban delirium of Dharavi.
We contemplated the enigma of modernity in silence.

All this motivated me to put history behind me and enter the present time and for this I am grateful for Benno Albrecht's invitation to describe Koenigsberger's legacy in Africa in a short text published for his exhibition, "Africa: Big Change Big Chance". Last but not least, I should also say that reading Carlo Ratti's book *Open Source Architecture* has led me to believe that the themes tackled in this research are of vital importance for architecture in the narrow sense of the term.

The formulation of the book is the result of all this, but its final guise is due to the intervention of Stefano Mandato, who by listening to the contents restored my faith in being able to organize everything fully, in a vivid and natural way.

In conclusion, everything seemed to have been outlined by means of text and drawings, and instead, at the very moment I write this, the photographer and architect Marco Introini is setting off for India. His artistic and documentary interpretative will serve to illustrate, through pictures of the tropical landscape, the universality of the Indian modern paradigm.

tropical costants

/

MAPS BY ANNA NURRA

The identification of parameters that link questions of geography, environment and climate with the presence of natural resources and the socio-political organization of the population has made it possible to define new horizons for the redistribution of wealth through a new way of thinking about infra-structure and public services.

These parameters came to be known as tro-pical constants, and were later adopted by all the pre-modern nations that, in transition toward modernity, chose to take an egalitarian and democratic path to development.

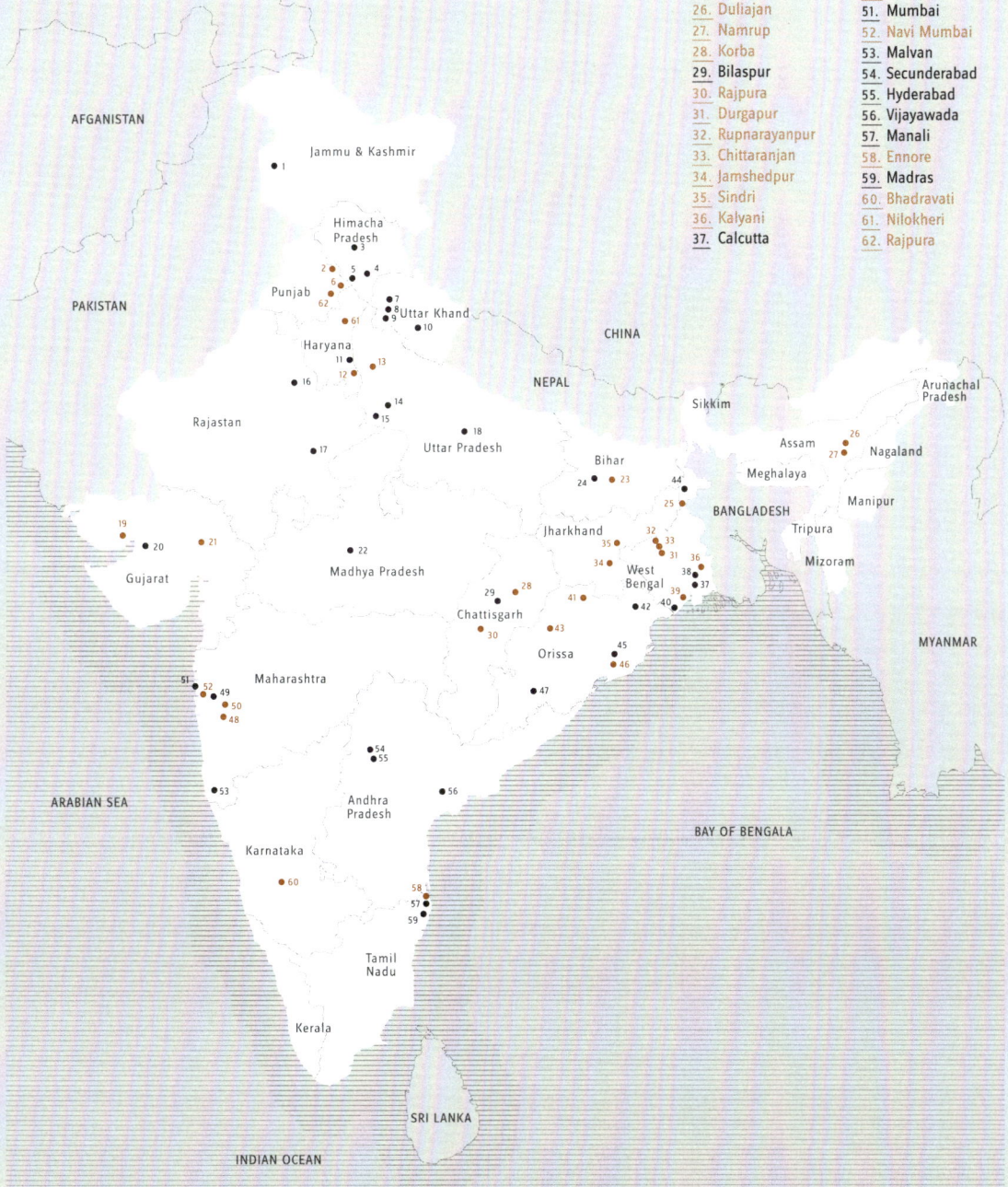

THE NEW TOWN PROTOCOL
INCLUDING THE MAIN CITIES

/

NEW TOWN
UPGRADED CITY

1. Gulmarg
2. Bhakra Nangal
3. Bilaspur
4. Shimla
5. Kasauli
6. Chandighar
7. Musso
8. Rishikesh
9. Haridwar
10. Ranikhet
11. New Dehli
12. Faridabad
13. New Okhla
14. Tundla
15. Agra
16. Khetri Nagar
17. Sawai Madhoupur
18. Lucknow
19. Gandhidham
20. Kandra
21. Gandhinagar
22. Bhopal
23. Barauni
24. New Patna
25. Farakka
26. Duliajan
27. Namrup
28. Korba
29. Bilaspur
30. Rajpura
31. Durgapur
32. Rupnarayanpur
33. Chittaranjan
34. Jamshedpur
35. Sindri
36. Kalyani
37. Calcutta
38. Barrackpore
39. Haldia
40. Digha
41. Rourkela
42. Kharagpur
43. Hirakund
44. Choudwar
45. Cuttak
46. Bhubaneswar
47. Koraput
48. Khadakvasla
49. Khopoli
50. Pimpri-Chichwad
51. Mumbai
52. Navi Mumbai
53. Malvan
54. Secunderabad
55. Hyderabad
56. Vijayawada
57. Manali
58. Ennore
59. Madras
60. Bhadravati
61. Nilokheri
62. Rajpura

AFGHANISTAN
PAKISTAN
Jammu & Kashmir
Himacha Pradesh
Punjab
Uttar Khand
Haryana
CHINA
NEPAL
Rajastan
Uttar Pradesh
Bihar
Sikkim
Arunachal Pradesh
Assam
Nagaland
Meghalaya
Manipur
BANGLADESH
Tripura
Mizoram
Gujarat
Madhya Pradesh
Jharkhand
West Bengal
Chattisgarh
Orissa
MYANMAR
Maharashtra
ARABIAN SEA
Andhra Pradesh
Karnataka
BAY OF BENGALA
Tamil Nadu
Kerala
SRI LANKA
INDIAN OCEAN

Indian Architecture Building Democracy

CLIMATIC ZONES

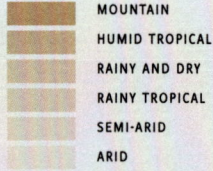

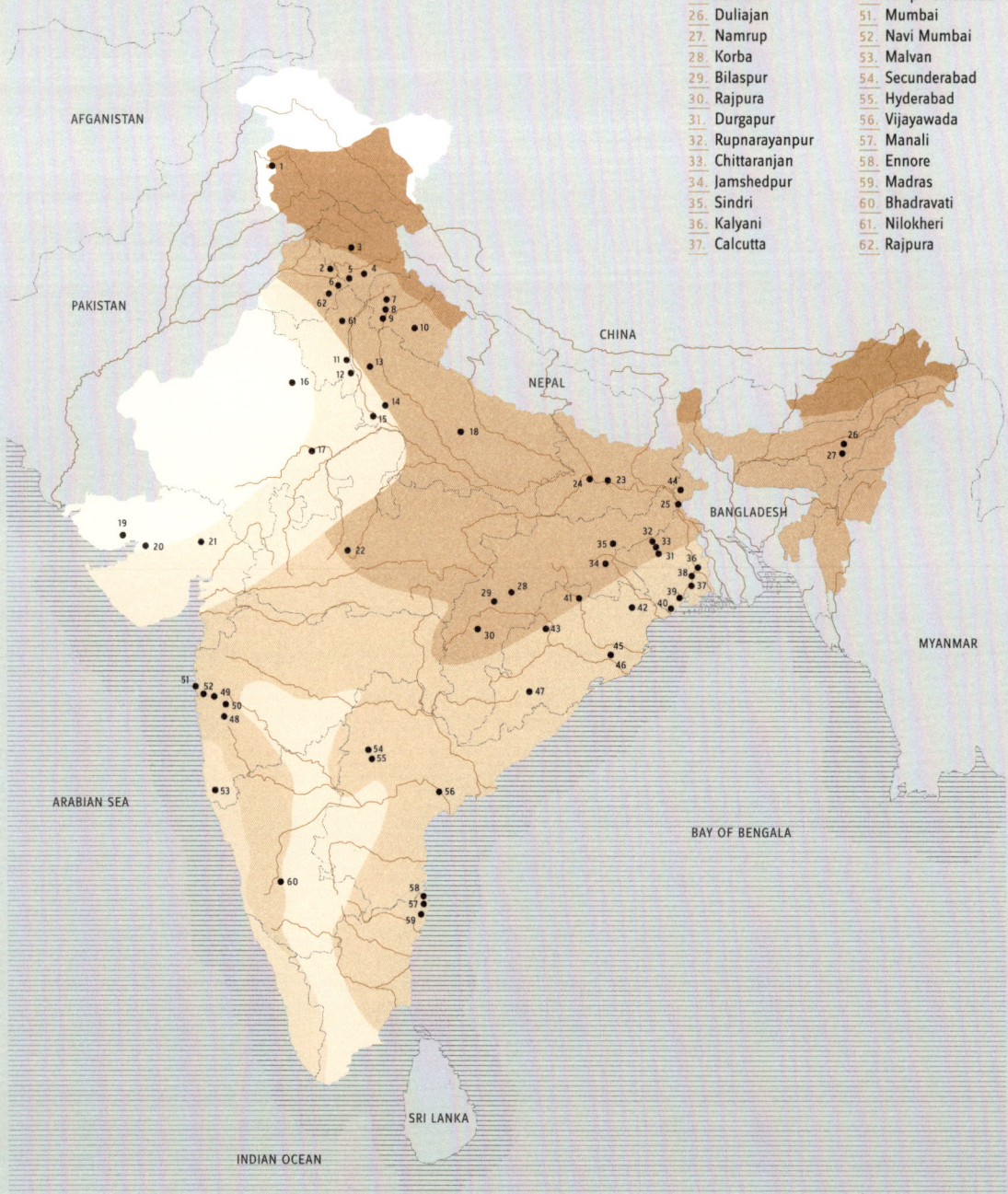

/

MOUNTAIN
HUMID TROPICAL
RAINY AND DRY
RAINY TROPICAL
SEMI-ARID
ARID

1. Gulmarg
2. Bhakra Nangal
3. Bilaspur
4. Shimla
5. Kasauli
6. Chandighar
7. Mussoorie
8. Rishikesh
9. Haridwar
10. Ranikhet
11. New Dehli
12. Faridabad

13. New Okhla
14. Tundla
15. Agra
16. Khetri Nagar
17. Sawai Madhoupur
18. Lucknow
19. Gandhidham
20. Kandra
21. Gandhinagar
22. Bhopal
23. Barauni
24. New Patna
25. Farakka
26. Duliajan
27. Namrup
28. Korba
29. Bilaspur
30. Rajpura
31. Durgapur
32. Rupnarayanpur
33. Chittaranjan
34. Jamshedpur
35. Sindri
36. Kalyani
37. Calcutta

38. Barrackpore
39. Haldia
40. Digha
41. Rourkela
42. Kharagpur
43. Hirakund
44. Choudwar
45. Cuttak
46. Bhubaneswar
47. Koraput
48. Khadakvasla
49. Khopoli
50. Pimpri-Chichwad
51. Mumbai
52. Navi Mumbai
53. Malvan
54. Secunderabad
55. Hyderabad
56. Vijayawada
57. Manali
58. Ennore
59. Madras
60. Bhadravati
61. Nilokheri
62. Rajpura

AFGANISTAN

PAKISTAN

CHINA

NEPAL

BANGLADESH

MYANMAR

ARABIAN SEA

BAY OF BENGALA

SRI LANKA

INDIAN OCEAN

WARM MODERNITY

AVERAGE ANNUAL PRECIPITATION

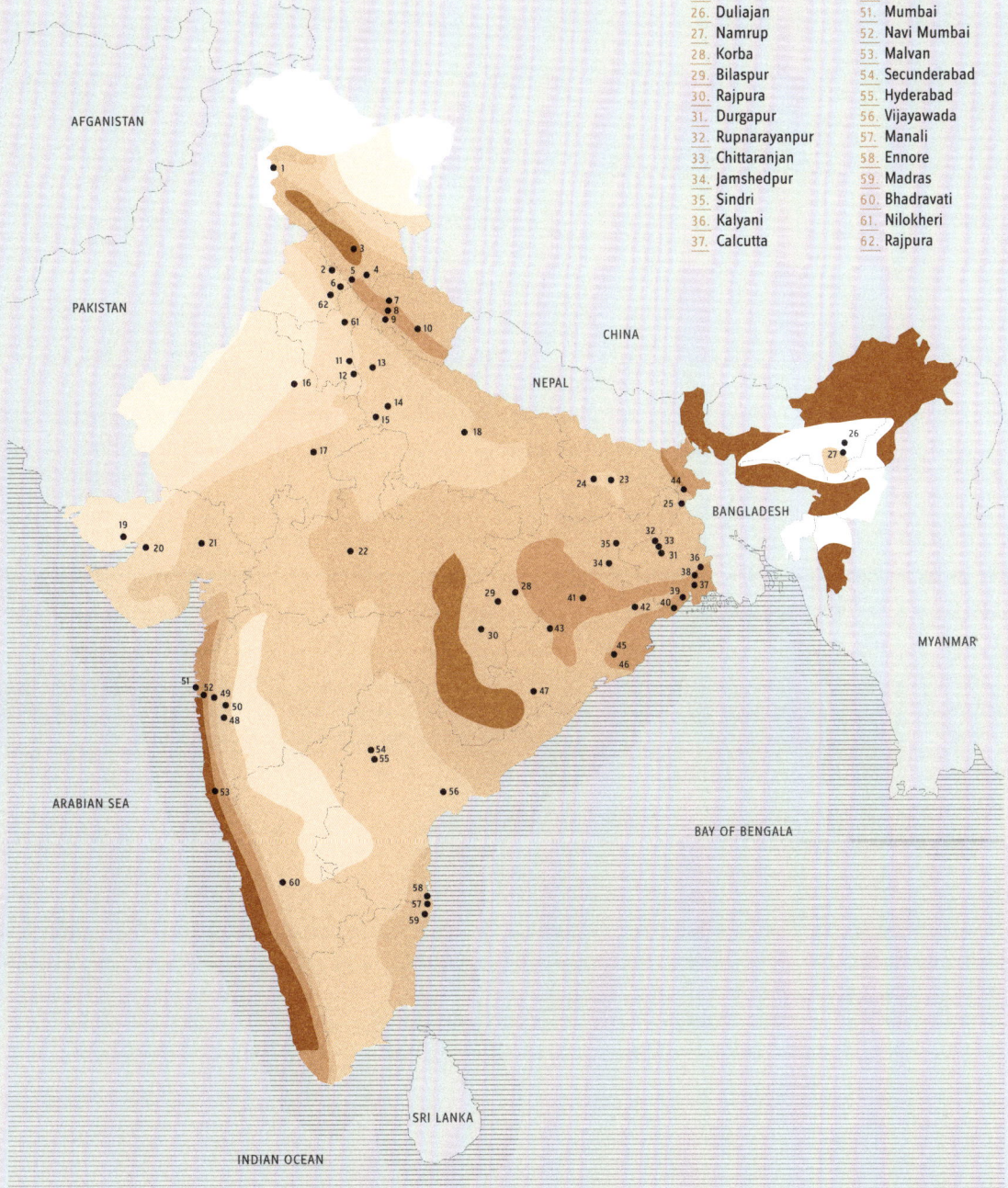

Legend:
- < 20 CM
- 20–40 CM
- 40–50 CM
- 60–100 CM
- 100–150 CM
- 150–250 CM
- > 250 CM

1. Gulmarg
2. Bhakra Nangal
3. Bilaspur
4. Shimla
5. Kasauli
6. Chandighar
7. Mussoorie
8. Rishikesh
9. Haridwar
10. Ranikhet
11. New Dehli
12. Faridabad
13. New Okhla
14. Tundla
15. Agra
16. Khetri Nagar
17. Sawai Madhoupur
18. Lucknow
19. Gandhidham
20. Kandra
21. Gandhinagar
22. Bhopal
23. Barauni
24. New Patna
25. Farakka
26. Duliajan
27. Namrup
28. Korba
29. Bilaspur
30. Rajpura
31. Durgapur
32. Rupnarayanpur
33. Chittaranjan
34. Jamshedpur
35. Sindri
36. Kalyani
37. Calcutta
38. Barrackpore
39. Haldia
40. Digha
41. Rourkela
42. Kharagpur
43. Hirakund
44. Choudwar
45. Cuttak
46. Bhubaneswar
47. Koraput
48. Khadakvasla
49. Khopoli
50. Pimpri-Chichwad
51. Mumbai
52. Navi Mumbai
53. Malvan
54. Secunderabad
55. Hyderabad
56. Vijayawada
57. Manali
58. Ennore
59. Madras
60. Bhadravati
61. Nilokheri
62. Rajpura

AFGANISTAN
PAKISTAN
CHINA
NEPAL
BANGLADESH
MYANMAR
ARABIAN SEA
BAY OF BENGALA
SRI LANKA
INDIAN OCEAN

Indian Architecture Building Democracy

AVERAGE ANNUAL TEMPERATURE

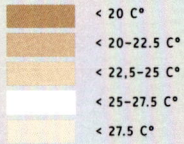

	< 20 C°
	< 20–22.5 C°
	< 22,5–25 C°
	< 25–27.5 C°
	< 27.5 C°

/

1.	Gulmarg	13.	New Okhla	38.	Barrackpore
2.	Bhakra Nangal	14.	Tundla	39.	Haldia
3.	Bilaspur	15.	Agra	40.	Digha
4.	Shimla	16.	Khetri Nagar	41.	Rourkela
5.	Kasauli	17.	Sawai Madhoupur	42.	Kharagpur
6.	Chandighar	18.	Lucknow	43.	Hirakund
7.	Mussoorie	19.	Gandhidham	44.	Choudwar
8.	Rishikesh	20.	Kandra	45.	Cuttak
9.	Haridwar	21.	Gandhinagar	46.	Bhubaneswar
10.	Ranikhet	22.	Bhopal	47.	Koraput
11.	New Dehli	23.	Barauni	48.	Khadakvasla
12.	Faridabad	24.	New Patna	49.	Khopoli
		25.	Farakka	50.	Pimpri-Chichwad
		26.	Duliajan	51.	Mumbai
		27.	Namrup	52.	Navi Mumbai
		28.	Korba	53.	Malvan
		29.	Bilaspur	54.	Secunderabad
		30.	Rajpura	55.	Hyderabad
		31.	Durgapur	56.	Vijayawada
		32.	Rupnarayanpur	57.	Manali
		33.	Chittaranjan	58.	Ennore
		34.	Jamshedpur	59.	Madras
		35.	Sindri	60.	Bhadravati
		36.	Kalyani	61.	Nilokheri
		37.	Calcutta	62.	Rajpura

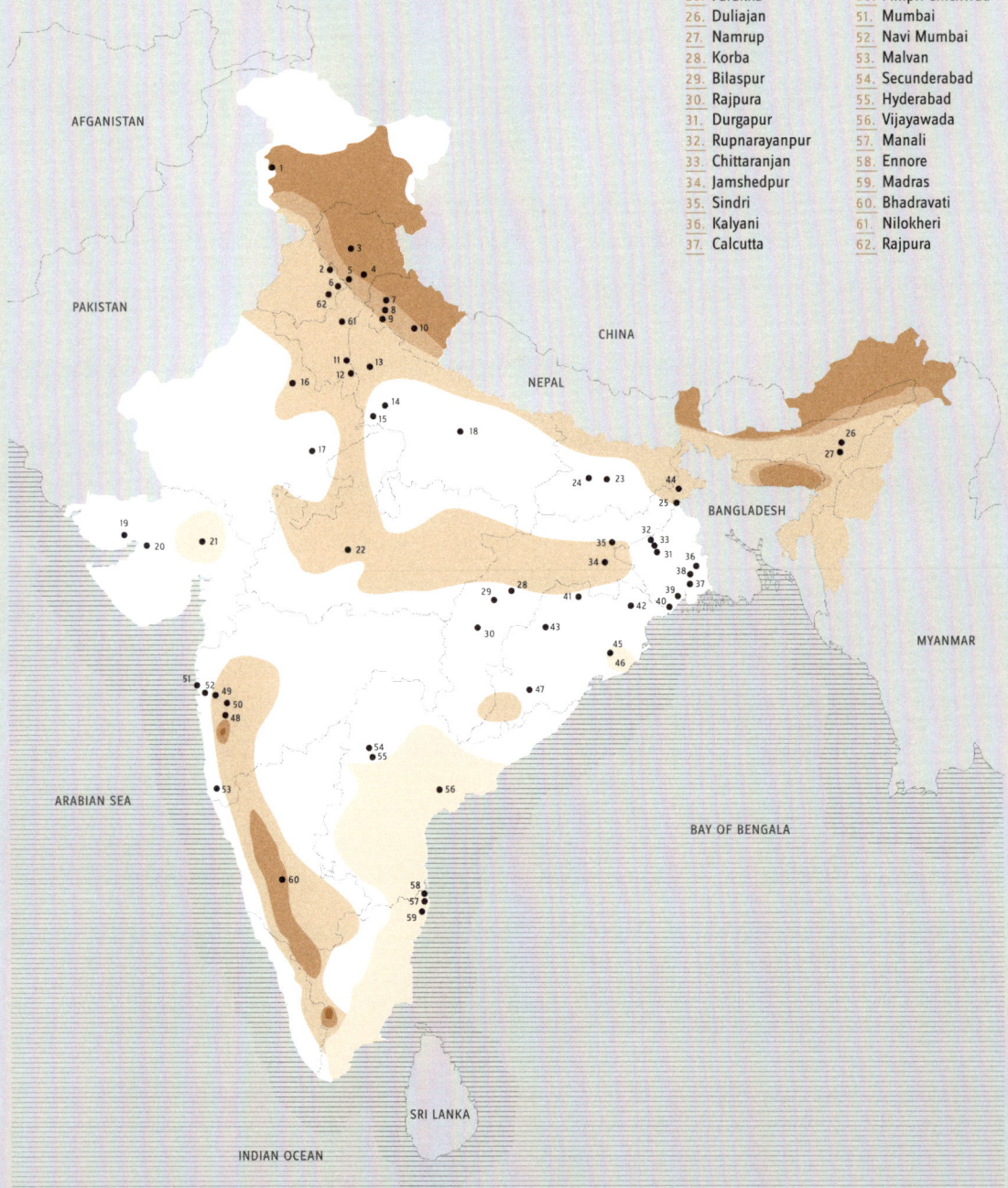

AFGHANISTAN

PAKISTAN

CHINA

NEPAL

BANGLADESH

MYANMAR

ARABIAN SEA

BAY OF BENGALA

SRI LANKA

INDIAN OCEAN

WARM MODERNITY

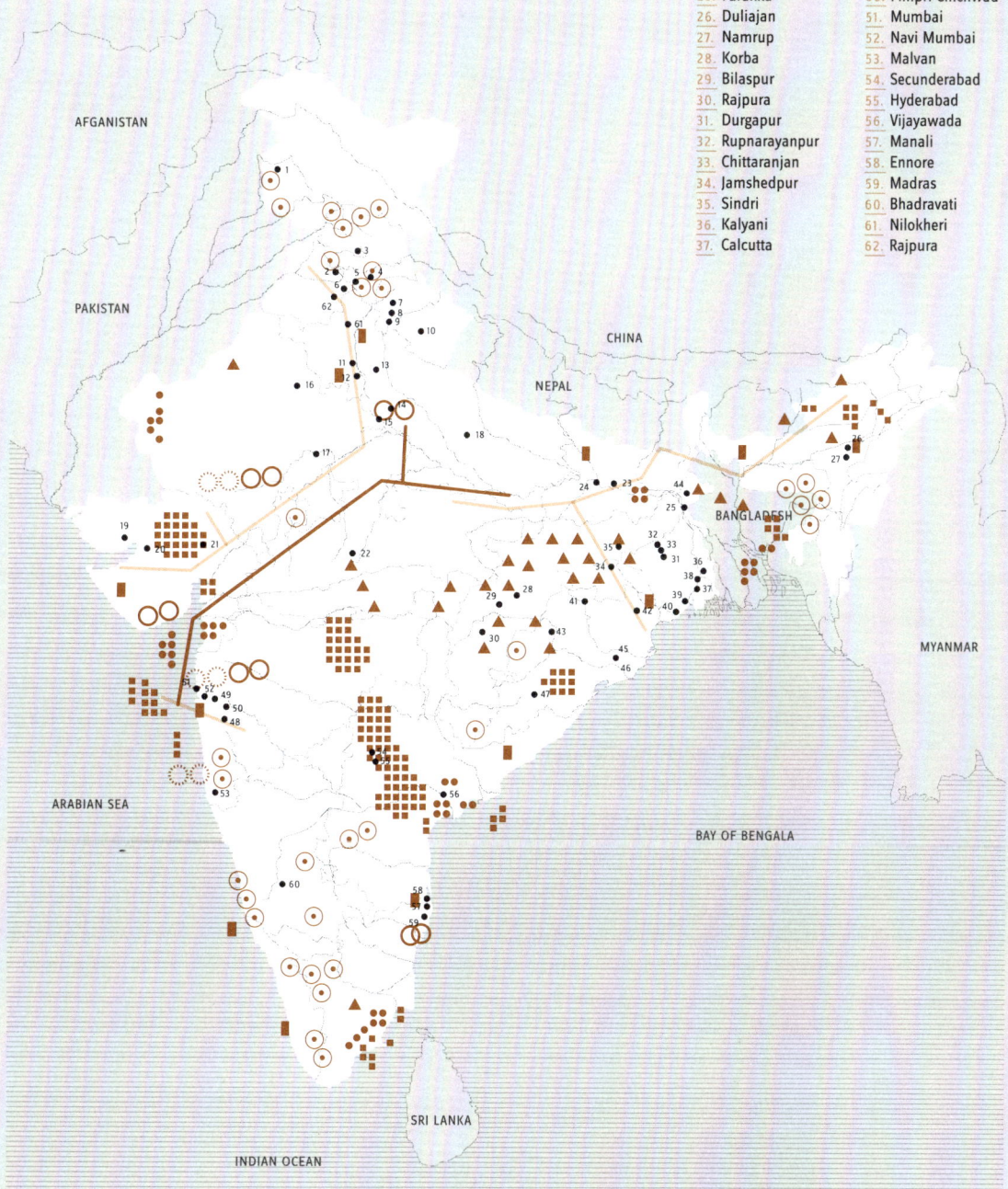

ENERGY
RESOURCES

/

Symbol	Legend
⊙	HYDROELECTRIC
◯	NUCLEAR OPERATING
⊙	NUCLEAR OPENING
▲	COAL RESERVES
▦	OIL RESERVES
⦂	GAS RESERVES
▪	OIL REFINERIES
⊥	OIL PIPELINES
⊤	GAS PIPELINES

1. Gulmarg
2. Bhakra Nangal
3. Bilaspur
4. Shimla
5. Kasauli
6. Chandighar
7. Mussoorie
8. Rishikesh
9. Haridwar
10. Ranikhet
11. New Dehli
12. Faridabad
13. New Okhla
14. Tundla
15. Agra
16. Khetri Nagar
17. Sawai Madhoupur
18. Lucknow
19. Gandhidham
20. Kandra
21. Gandhinagar
22. Bhopal
23. Barauni
24. New Patna
25. Farakka
26. Duliajan
27. Namrup
28. Korba
29. Bilaspur
30. Rajpura
31. Durgapur
32. Rupnarayanpur
33. Chittaranjan
34. Jamshedpur
35. Sindri
36. Kalyani
37. Calcutta
38. Barrackpore
39. Haldia
40. Digha
41. Rourkela
42. Kharagpur
43. Hirakund
44. Choudwar
45. Cuttak
46. Bhubaneswar
47. Koraput
48. Khadakvasla
49. Khopoli
50. Pimpri-Chichwad
51. Mumbai
52. Navi Mumbai
53. Malvan
54. Secunderabad
55. Hyderabad
56. Vijayawada
57. Manali
58. Ennore
59. Madras
60. Bhadravati
61. Nilokheri
62. Rajpura

AFGANISTAN

PAKISTAN

CHINA

NEPAL

BANGLADESH

MYANMAR

ARABIAN SEA

BAY OF BENGALA

SRI LANKA

INDIAN OCEAN

Indian Architecture Building Democracy

POVERTY RATE PERCENTAGE

	35–40
	30–35
	25–30
	20–25
	15–20
	10–15
	1–10

1. Gulmarg
2. Bhakra Nangal
3. Bilaspur
4. Shimla
5. Kasauli
6. Chandighar
7. Mussoorie
8. Rishikesh
9. Haridwar
10. Ranikhet
11. New Dehli
12. Faridabad
13. New Okhla
14. Tundla
15. Agra
16. Khetri Nagar
17. Sawai Madhoupur
18. Lucknow
19. Gandhidham
20. Kandra
21. Gandhinagar
22. Bhopal
23. Barauni
24. New Patna
25. Farakka
26. Duliajan
27. Namrup
28. Korba
29. Bilaspur
30. Rajpura
31. Durgapur
32. Rupnarayanpur
33. Chittaranjan
34. Jamshedpur
35. Sindri
36. Kalyani
37. Calcutta
38. Barrackpore
39. Haldia
40. Digha
41. Rourkela
42. Kharagpur
43. Hirakund
44. Choudwar
45. Cuttak
46. Bhubaneswar
47. Koraput
48. Khadakvasla
49. Khopoli
50. Pimpri-Chichwad
51. Mumbai
52. Navi Mumbai
53. Malvan
54. Secunderabad
55. Hyderabad
56. Vijayawada
57. Manali
58. Ennore
59. Madras
60. Bhadravati
61. Nilokheri
62. Rajpura

AFGANISTAN

PAKISTAN

CHINA

NEPAL

BANGLADESH

MYANMAR

ARABIAN SEA

BAY OF BENGALA

SRI LANKA

INDIAN OCEAN

WARM MODERNITY

BEST PRACTICES

/

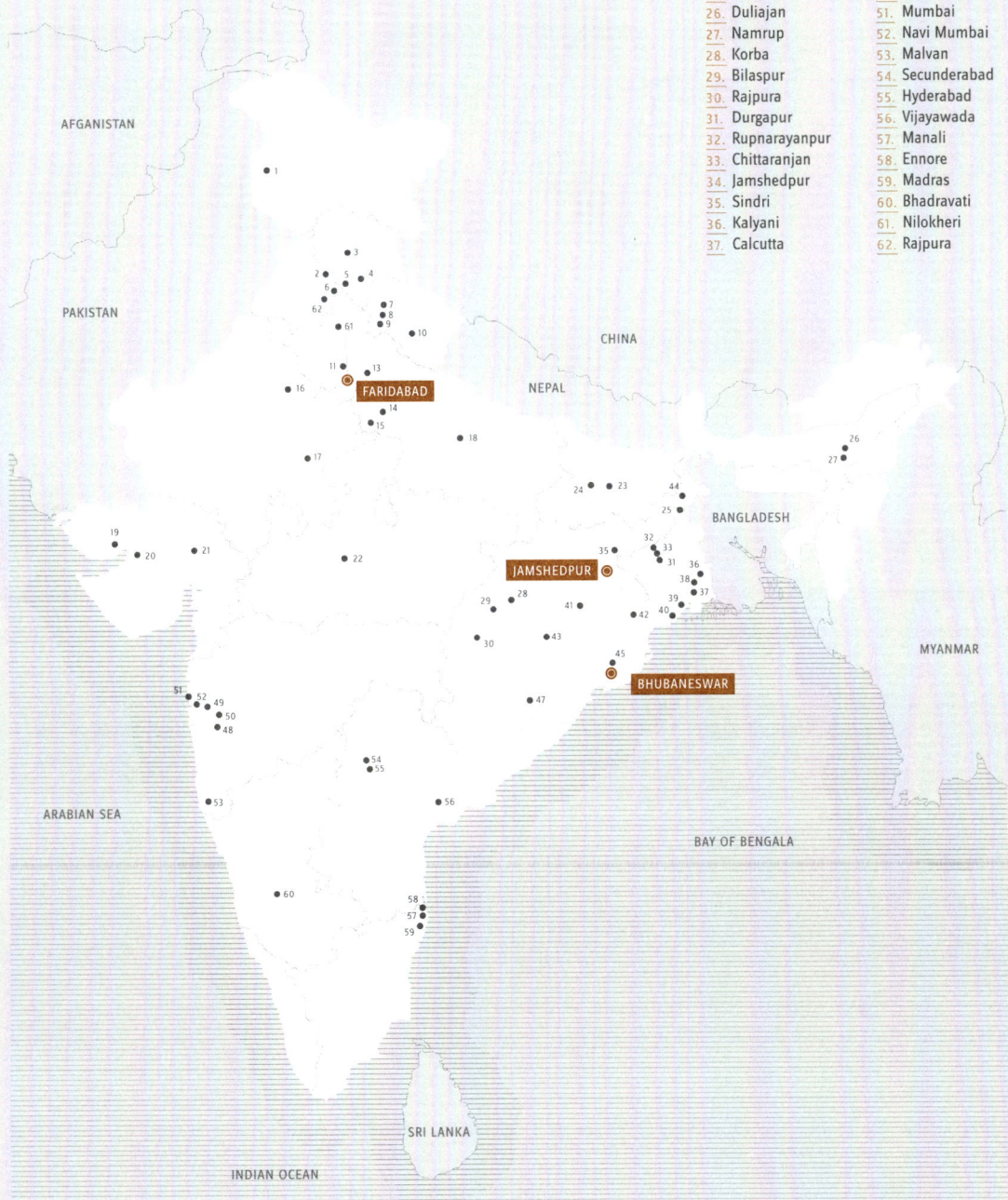

1. Gulmarg
2. Bhakra Nangal
3. Bilaspur
4. Shimla
5. Kasauli
6. Chandighar
7. Mussoorie
8. Rishikesh
9. Haridwar
10. Ranikhet
11. New Dehli
12. Faridabad
13. New Okhla
14. Tundla
15. Agra
16. Khetri Nagar
17. Sawai Madhoupur
18. Lucknow
19. Gandhidham
20. Kandra
21. Gandhinagar
22. Bhopal
23. Barauni
24. New Patna
25. Farakka
26. Duliajan
27. Namrup
28. Korba
29. Bilaspur
30. Rajpura
31. Durgapur
32. Rupnarayanpur
33. Chittaranjan
34. Jamshedpur
35. Sindri
36. Kalyani
37. Calcutta
38. Barrackpore
39. Haldia
40. Digha
41. Rourkela
42. Kharagpur
43. Hirakund
44. Choudwar
45. Cuttak
46. Bhubaneswar
47. Koraput
48. Khadakvasla
49. Khopoli
50. Pimpri-Chichwad
51. Mumbai
52. Navi Mumbai
53. Malvan
54. Secunderabad
55. Hyderabad
56. Vijayawada
57. Manali
58. Ennore
59. Madras
60. Bhadravati
61. Nilokheri
62. Rajpura

Indian Architecture Building Democracy

WARM MODERNITY

IMPORTING MODERNITY

architects
of interest

/

It can be said that an important chapter in modern architecture and city planning found a synthesis and a practical application in India under the guidance of Otto Koenigsberger. The principal ideas introduced into India at the moment of independence and Partition were based on European models.

The guidelines of the band town pattern, the urban paradigm outlined by Otto Koenigsberger for modern towns of medium and small dimensions, were derived from his studies and training in Berlin, at a time when an attempt was being made to find a synthesis between the model of the garden city and that of the Siedlungen through contributions from Ernst May, Hermann Jansen, Fritz Schumacher, Theodor Fischer, Heinrich Tessenow, Ebenezer Howard and Raymond Unwin.

EBENEZER HOWARD
1850–1928

/

SELECTED PROJECTS

1913   Consultant for Letchworth
Garden City

1920   Consultant for Welwyn
Garden City

EBENEZER HOWARD'S GARDEN CITY

As envisaged in Ebenezer Howard's drawings of the Garden City, the proto-col for new towns of medium and small size set out to reduce the growing congestion of big cities through a low-density grouping of detached houses linked together by services and the tertiary sector, and to integrate it with the countryside in order to provide the environmental advantages of a direct link with the territory.

On the one hand, in fact, the population was accustomed to living in the open air and its extended families were used to sharing domestic spaces, while on the other the backward conditions of a rural society raised questions about modernization. There were, in fact, two currents in the de-bate within the country: the Gandhian one, which hypothesized an agrarian modernity and production based on subsistence farming, and the Nehruvian one, which proposed a model based on industrialization in accordance with theories of economic development.

Outlining a modern rural and urban paradigm would have reconci-led and blended the positions of the two founding fathers of the country.

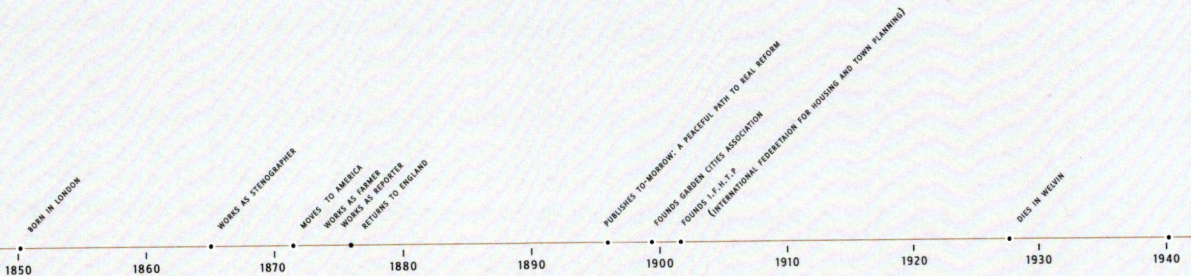

BORN IN LONDON

WORKS TO STENOGRAPHER

MOVES TO AMERICA
WORKS AS FARMER
WORKS AS REPORTER
RETURNS TO ENGLAND

PUBLISHES TO-MORROW: A PEACEFUL PATH TO REAL REFORM

FOUNDS GARDEN CITIES ASSOCIATION

FOUNDS I.F.H.T.P.
(INTERNATIONAL FEDERATION FOR HOUSING AND TOWN PLANNING)

DIES IN WELWYN

1850   1860   1870   1880   1890   1900   1910   1920   1930   1940

RAYMOND UNWIN
1863–1940

/

SELECTED PROJECTS

1902 Plan of New Earswick village

1903 Plan of Letchwort garden city

1905 Plan of Hampstee garden city

1907 Plan of Brentham suburb, London

1930 Consultant for London's Plan

In 1903 Raymond Unwin and Barry Parker drew up the plans for Letchworth, after winning the competition staged by the company called First Garden City, Ltd. In 1919 he was appointed Chief Architect to the British Ministry of Health, founded that same year, a post whose name was later changed to Chief Technical Officer for Housing and Town Planning.

One of the specific questions on which he focused was the development of a system for the design of houses that could be built cheaply and rapidly, while ensuring that the internal spaces met the new standards of family privacy and gardens were included at the front and back. His ability became clear to all during the period of the Great War, when he succeeded in applying his method of construction in a convincing and systematic manner.

This approach to urban planning, which married industrialization to new living standards, formed the basis of the Indian protocol.

| 1850 | 1860 | 1870 | 1880 | 1890 | 1900 | 1910 | 1920 | 1930 | 1940 |

BORN IN ROTTERDAM
MOVES TO LONDON
STUDIES IN OXFORD
MOVES TO MANCHESTER
MEMBER OF ART AND CRAFT MOVEMENT
PUBLICS THE ART OF BUILDING A HOME WITH RICHARD BARRY PARKER
MOVES TO LONDON
TOWN PLANNING INSTITUTE
CHIEF ARCHITECT
MINISTRY OF HEALTH
CHIEF TECHNICAL OFFICER HOUSING AND TOWN PLANNING
MOVES TO U.S.A
PROFESSOR IN URBAN PLANNING COLUMBIA UNIVERSITY
DIES IN LONDON

HEINRICH TESSENOW
1876–1950

/

SELECTED PROJECTS

1906   Masterplan Hellerau, Dresden, Germany

1910-12   Jaques-Dalcroze Institute, Hellerau, Germany

1917   Settlement Siedlungen in Vienna, Austria

1920   Public Garden in Vienna, Austria

1921-24   Housing for the Staff of a Brewery in Rannersdorf, Austria

1928-29   Siedlungen in Berlin-Zehlendorf, Germany

1929   House Tessenow in Berlin, Germany

1940-41   Residential development for the Junkers Aircraft and MotorSystem in Magdeburg

THE CITY OF ARTISANS CONCEIVED BY HEINRICH TESSENOW FOR KARL SCHMIDT

For Heinrich Tessenow the city of Hellerau was the pretext for a reflection on the secular space linked to the new industrial technology. Among the questions still relevant to the present day tackled in his plan, perhaps the most topical is the one concerning the need to find a conceptual platform that would integrate the short timescale of human life and the long one of industrial machinery in urban space. He devised a remarkable solution, deciding that the rhythm of movement in space was what natural and artificial life had in common.

On the basis of a personal choice, community life was coordinated in accordance with principles of natural coexistence and material cooperation. In this way the buildings symbolic of power were slightly decentralized: those of industry (in that case, the client), those of government and politics (at a time of radical ideological conflict) and, last but far from least, those of the religious institutions. In India after Partition and still in our own day, the question of the possibility of using space to build tolerance is a very real one, so that even today the planning of secular space linked to the time of its uses seems paradigmatic.

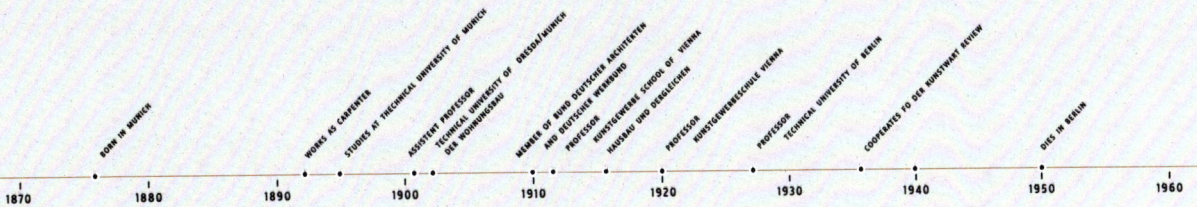

1870		1880		1890		1900		1910		1920		1930		1940		1950		1960

BORN IN MUNICH
WORKS AS CARPENTER
STUDIES AT TECHNICAL UNIVERSITY OF MUNICH
ASSISTENT PROFESSOR TECHNICAL UNIVERSITY OF DRESDEN/MUNICH
DER WOHNUNGSBAU
MEMBER OF BUND DEUTSCHER ARCHITEKTEN AND DEUTSCHER WERKBUND
PROFESSOR KUNSTGEWERBE SCHOOL OF VIENNA
HAUSBAU UND DERGLEICHEN
PROFESSOR KUNSTGEWERBESCHULE VIENNA
PROFESSOR TECHNICAL UNIVERSITY OF BERLIN
COOPERATES FO DER KUNSTWART REVIEW
DIES IN BERLIN

ERNST MAY
1886–1970

/

SELECTED PROJECTS

1921   Masterplan Breslaw, Poland
1925   Masterplan, Frankfurt, Germany
1930-33 Masterplan, Magnitogorsk, Stalinsk, URSS
1934-37 Farmer near Mount Meru, Arusha, Tanzania
1937   Kenwood Houses, Nairobi, Kenya
1940-42 Interned in South Africa
1945-51 House for an African Family, Delamere Flats, Nairobi, Kenia
1955   Extension of Hamburg, Germany

ERNST MAY'S FUNCTIONALIST TOWN ON THE OUTSKIRTS OF FRANKFURT

Following the experience of the Weissenhof, Ernst May planned housing developments on the basis of codes referring to a new quality of life, setting detached houses alongside row houses and apartment blocks so that they could accommodate different social classes and encourage a mixed use of the town. In fact commercial zones were planned at the ends of the districts as locations for small local stores, libraries, post offices and institutional services, and above all to provide access to railroads or surface rapid transit systems. It was a question of planning multifunctional urban zones with a complex use for a city open to daily life. The last element introduced into India through the New Towns Protocol was, indeed, the study of a complex neighborhood unit.

The idea of the neighborhood unit was developed in parallel by Clarence Perry in 1929 and was used as the basis for expansion of the city. It hinged on six fundamental points: size, boundaries, open spaces, spaces for services, local stores and an internal system of streets. These same points were organized in India in such a way as to allow them to be constructed and completed in successive phases, a process that later came to be known as incremental.

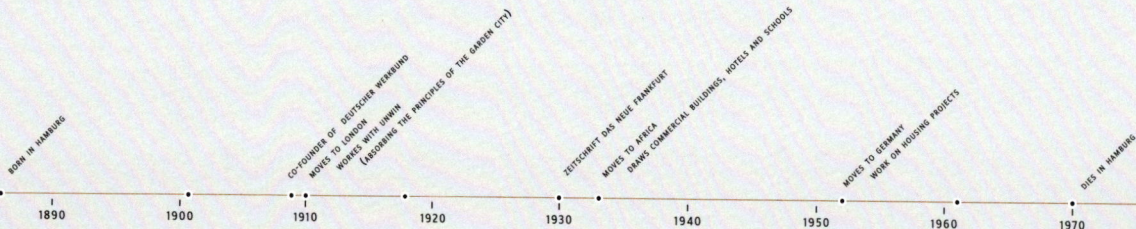

BORN IN HAMBURG

CO-FOUNDER OF DEUTSCHER WERKBUND
MOVES TO LONDON
WORKES WITH UNWIN
(ABSORBING THE PRINCIPLES OF THE GARDEN CITY)

ZEITSCHRIFT DAS NEUE FRANKFURT
MOVES TO AFRICA
DRAWS COMMERCIAL BUILDINGS, HOTELS AND SCHOOLS

MOVES TO GERMANY
WORK ON HOUSING PROJECTS

DIES IN HAMBURG

1880   1890   1900   1910   1920   1930   1940   1950   1960   1970   1980

WARM MODERNITY

PATRICK GEDDES

1854–1932

/

SELECTED PROJECTS

1890   Cities in Exibition, Edimburg, London, Dublino Belfast, Gand, Madras

1915-19   Town planning reports, India

1919   Studies for Dublin city, with Unwin
Master Plan, Jerusalem

1925   Master Plan, Tel Aviv

THE STUDIES OF PATRICK GEDDES

Patrick Geddes had fostered in India the idea of planning as a great game played out between inhabitants and planners, to be activated on the level of the city. Society and city were regarded as cellular bodies whose growth was interrelated.

The neighborhood unit, conceived on the basis of this analysis, was later chosen by Koenigsberger as the ideal place in which to bring about a full correspondence between action and educational spiral, i.e. the territory in which the citizen could learns the rules of democratic life through cooperation and thus play a part in public life.

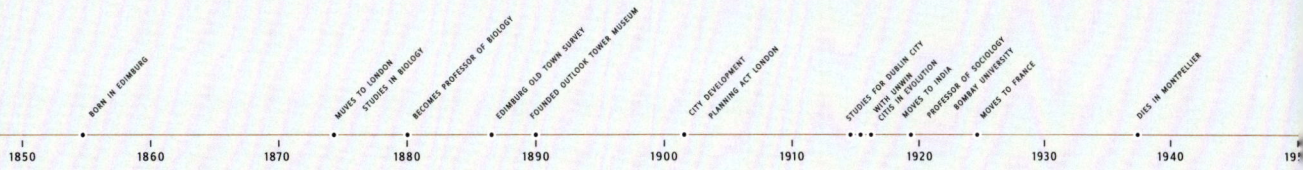

BORN IN EDIMBURG   MOVES TO LONDON   STUDIES IN BIOLOGY   BECOMES PROFESSOR OF BIOLOGY   EDIMBURG OLD TOWN SURVEY   FOUNDED OUTLOOK TOWER MUSEUM   CITY DEVELOPMENT   PLANNING ACT LONDON   STUDIES FOR DUBLIN CITY   WITH UNWIN   CITIS IN EVOLUTION   MOVES TO INDIA   PROFESSOR OF SOCIOLOGY   BOMBAY UNIVERSITY   MOVES TO FRANCE   DIES IN MONTPELLIER

| 1850 | 1860 | 1870 | 1880 | 1890 | 1900 | 1910 | 1920 | 1930 | 1940 | 195 |

Indian Architecture Building Democracy

OTTO KOENIGSBERGER
1908–1999

/

SELECTED PROJECTS

1943-45 Dining Hall at Indian
        Institute of Science,
        Bangalore, India
1944-45 Master Plan, Jamshedpur,
        India
1948-51 Master Plan, Rajpura
        and Nilokheri, India
1948   Master Plan, Bhubaneswar,
        India
1949   Master Plan, Faridabad,
        India
1950   Master Plan, Chandigarh,
        India
1950-51 Master Plan, Gandhidam,
        India

THE SENSIBILITY OF OTTO KOENIGSBERGER

Otto Koenigsberger, an architect and city planner who had fled from a Nazi and racist Germany, had arrived in India after a brief stay in Egypt to obtain a doctorate in archeology. Thus he was a person who had cultivated a feeling for the history and cultural heritage of non-European contexts. His work in Bangalore and Jamshedpur made him the key man to oversee the Indian planning of new towns and cities.

So he was called on to draw up a protocol designed to bring India into the modern era. And it was in these circumstances that he came up with the band town pattern, creating, de facto, the precondition for a modern Indian paradigm.

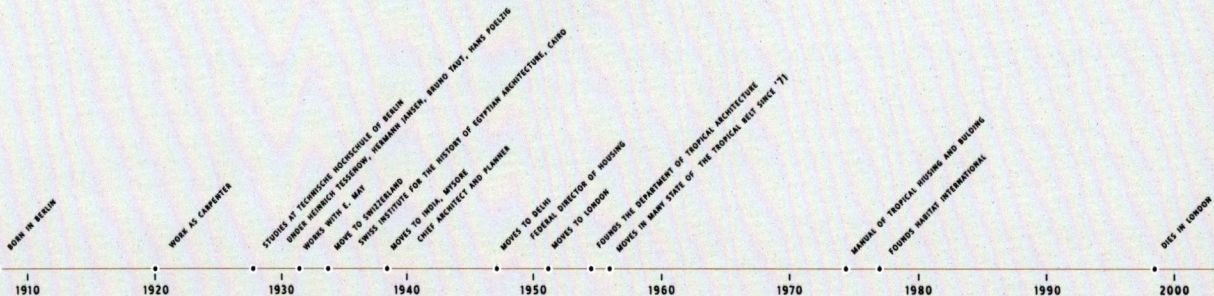

BORN IN BERLIN

WORK AS CARPENTER

STUDIES AT TECHNISCHE HOCHSCHULE OF BERLIN
UNDER HEINRICH TESSENOW, BRUNO TAUT, HANS POELZIG

WORKS WITH E. MAY

MOVE TO SWITZERLAND
SWISS INSTITUTE FOR THE HISTORY OF EGYPTIAN ARCHITECTURE, CAIRO

MOVES TO INDIA, MYSORE
CHIEF ARCHITECT AND PLANNER

MOVES TO DELHI
FEDERAL DIRECTOR OF HOUSING

MOVES TO LONDON

FOUNDS THE DEPARTMENT OF TROPICAL ARCHITECTURE
MOVES IN MANY STATE OF THE TROPICAL BELT SINCE '71

MANUAL OF TROPICAL HOUSING AND BUILDING
FOUNDS HABITAT INTERNATIONAL

DIES IN LONDON

| 1910 | 1920 | 1930 | 1940 | 1950 | 1960 | 1970 | 1980 | 1990 | 2000 |

WARM MODERNITY

THE NEW INDIAN PARADIGM: THE DEFINITION OF THE MODERN TROPICAL LANDSCAPE

/

MADDALENA D'ALFONSO

The Importance of the Case
–

Every age has its revolution and every history is the child of its time. This is why their stories have to be told. I believe, as do many, that to plan for the future it is necessary to rediscover the past.

The story told in this book is that of a little-known chapter in the developments that link architecture to the construction of the city of human rights: the city with a social and democratic matrix.

I think that this is a point of fundamental importance to an understanding of the questions that are raised with regard to contemporary urban design and that have to be tackled by any architect. Urgent and cogent problems, given that the city is today the principal form of human settlement, constantly growing in size and increasingly spontaneous in character. Questions of architecture, since this is the discipline that is specifically concerned with space and its design: from the macro-scale to the working scale, which we insiders like to call the scale of detail. Unknowns that need to be discussed, as the profession and discipline of architecture is faced with an uncertainty about its role that is due, in my opinion, not solely to a crisis in identity and in political values. Rather it is the product of a conscious and mature approach to the significance of designing and planning and to the necessity for active participation by the people who are going to live in the places or at least build them.

If for no other reason, because of that "necessary participation" in the realization of collective works, such as urban ones, or because of that "participation by necessity" in the construction of cumulative structures, like the informal areas of shanty towns and slums, as they are still called. Names that are quite unsuited to an understanding of the real process of their birth and their living form and which I therefore prefer to define as spontaneous built-up areas.

This story is one that surprisingly has unfolded outside the territory which has historically seen a conscious and deliberate focus on the link between the city and rights, developed over the course of history through the construction of public space, to be used to meet collective needs, hold religious and pagan rituals, stage temporary markets and festivals and for the self-representation of the separate powers: Europe. Instead the setting for this chapter, necessary to an understanding of the modern and contemporary city, has been India since 1945, following the country's process of independence from the United Kingdom and its Partition—the division of the territory of the Indian subcontinent between India and Pakistan (subsequently divided in turn into Pakistan and Bangladesh).

Given the urgent need for a profound change in the balance of the nation, the city was chosen by J. Nehru, M.K. Gandhi and the country's elite as the hub of a general political transformation that would involve and touch all sectors, from social aspects, anchored to a remote past, to those of production (agricultural, artisan and industrial), culminating in the assessment and redistribution of wealth on a geographical, and thus territorial and topographical basis. In other words the faith in the guiding role played by cities and architecture was confirmed.

The Relativity of the Case
–

The term "principle of relativity" is generically used to refer to the changes that have to be applied to the description of phenomena that occur in the passage between two frames of reference in motion relative to one another. To describe change in a complex phenomenon, in fact, parts of the phenomenon have to be isolated, even though their transformation is due to a wider context. If we consider this principle to be true then we must also admit that where there is change in one part, there will inevitably have been at least an alteration of the whole. [2] The same principle will help us to understand some of the most important decisions taken in India in order to modernize the country. These decisions, moreover, had a decisive influence on the course that would be taken by architecture and urban planning in the future.

The geopolitical situation at the time of India's independence was in the midst of its first systematic modern transformation, the one determined by the readjustment of international balances of power following the Second World War.
In this context it was in India that the conditions required for the definition of new urban paradigms arose. In fact the absence of conflict on the national territory, together with the increasing migration of the population into cities, permitted the emergence of a specific need and a place in which to come up with a synthesis and adaptation of the reflection on the modern city that had begun in Britain and Germany after the First World War.
The pioneering work of Patrick Geddes and his theories on the city and town planning, expressed in the book Cities in Evolution (1915) [3] found, during his stay in India from 1914 to 1924, a new and unusual field of inquiry. But later it was chiefly the efforts made by Otto Koenigsberger [4] from 1939 onward as Chief Architect of the Public Works Department in Mysore and as urban planner for corporate houses that made a new approach to the application of urban and social theories possible. [5]
It was extremely important, for the India of that

time, to reflect on the relationship between organization of the state and territory, social organization and urban design, representation of the new socialist and democratic political system and the construction of a future and of a new and up-to-date cultural elite, a process in which the recourse to new and multidisciplinary figures, like that of the urbanist architect, was indispensable. [6] It was in these circumstances that, despite being a foreigner, a man with the background of Otto Koenigsberger, the pupil of such great exponents of the modern German movement of avant-garde architecture as E. May, H. Poelzig, B. Taut and H. Tessenow and trained in Berlin at the extraordinary time of the reflections that emerged from the conferences of the MARS Group [7] (where an attempt was made to combine the utopian idea of the Garden City with the advantages of the German Siedlungen), was considered the ideal person to draw up and coordinate the Protocol for the New Town of Modern Foundation [8] (later known as the New Towns Protocol). And he was given a position that would be the envy of any self-respecting architect and city planner, Federal Director of Housing and Planning at the Ministry of Health in New Delhi. [9]

The Universality of the Case
–

The complicated history of Indian city planning as it took shape under the auspices of a newborn democracy and the shadow of the ill-omened division between Hindu and Muslim states was also the fruit of an unexpected worldwide ideological and idealistic debate that involved a number of prominent figures, not just Nehru, Gandhi, Tagore and Ambedkar but also Tito, Sukarno and Nasser.
In fact it was an extraordinary period in which countries on the fringes tried to find means of development and processes of evolution that could be adapted to conditions of profound underdevelopment in all sectors, despite an enormous wealth of traditions, culture and potential resources.

Given the rapidity of liberation and the apprehension over the possibilities of extremist sedition, therefore, there was a need for international support for the effort to introduce policies of social planning rooted in regional and urban reorganization of the vast and variegated territory of India.

Thus it was considered opportune to sidestep the onerous pacts imposed by both fronts of the Cold War and inaugurate instead a new and different alliance between countries whose needs were proving to be of quite another nature: distinguishing itself from both the Western and capitalist First World and the Soviet and socialist Second World, therefore, India became involved in the birth of the Third World, whose mixed interests oscillated between a natural inclination toward a socialist vision and the introduction of a free market out of necessity.

On the one hand, in fact, the advantages of long-term planning and protectionism in defense of domestic production and reserves following colonial despoliation were obvious, while on the other the benefits of a free market through which the population could determine the new course of its personal and collective history were equally evident.

The protocol of new towns proved to be a suitable means of solving a range of problems: reorganizing the territory in which they would be inserted, implementing a new social order built from scratch, creating civic spaces of coexistence and interreligious and interracial tolerance, modernizing systems of production and transport, representing the new authority based on democratic representation and introducing new relations between traditional structures and modern ones. In short, defining circumscribed places that could present a concise vision of the country's possible new course: that of a modern and democratic India. [10]

So in India a particular version of modernity was developed, whose application was the fruit of a totally unique alchemy between Western models and Indian cultural practices.

While in architecture of Western derivation a set of codes has been established that have inseparably linked modernity to an aesthetic image, through the architectural and urban experience that has unfolded in India it is possible to rediscover how fundamental aspects of modernity are instead linked to design practices that we would define as virtuous today. They have come to constitute a precise architectural and urban grammar free from any feeling of nostalgia and focusing an affectionate gaze on the future instead. The nostalgic sentiment of modernity, in fact, has been formalized in a language of mo-

dernist and international architecture summed up in magnificent designs by a highly cultured elite, [11] but its opposite side, the nostalgic dream of futurism, has been vulgarized by groups of insiders and spread through stereotyped formulas that can be repeated anywhere, or in the best of cases through globalized urban models. [12]

In India, by contrast, a dynamic movement has emerged that privileges and exploits the processual aspects of the design of architecture, of architectural construction and of active participation in the constitution and life of the city. This vision in fact has created the conditions for a separation between the aesthetics of classical modernity and modern democratic ethics, producing a set of sociopolitical strategies in architecture. At that precise moment in history, in the underdeveloped regions of the world, it was for the most part a question of implementing, through the participation of the population, new constitutional spaces: for work, education, the health service, democratic representation, leisure. They were, in fact, assigned a programmatic role of educating and improving health that harked back to the progressive and liberal optimism once typical of Europe.

I believe that these premises are at the root of the cultural crisis in contemporary architectural thinking, above all as far as the philosophy of the language and grammar of architecture are concerned. What becomes evident here is the priority of identifying a space whose uses and frequentation are determined in a participatory manner, making it possible to contemplate a marginalization of its aesthetic qualities. Indeed the concept has emerged that participation and democratic use ennobles a space in and of itself. Taken as a whole, these considerations make the Indian case indispensable to the study and understanding of participatory architecture and planning, and lay the foundations for a conscious and critical reformulation of modern architecture.

The Historical Case
–

When the Indian subcontinent gained its independence, in 1947, the territory underwent Partition, i.e. its division between sovereign states (at the time

India and Pakistan) on a religious ethnic basis. As a result of the sudden outbreak of bloody conflicts, up to seventeen million refugees crossed the new frontiers in both directions. It was the first mass migration of people in modern times, followed with bated breath by the whole world and documented by the incredible pictures taken by the American war correspondent and photographer Margaret Bourke-White for the weekly Life.

Craftsmen, stockbreeders, small-scale entrepreneurs, farmers, storekeepers, marginal religious communities, traders and every kind of small or large organization, family-based or cooperative in nature, and in general anyone linked to manufacturing activities or at the bottom of discriminatory social hierarchies, were obliged to make a journey to a new world, knowing only the one they had left behind and only being able to imagine the one they would have to rebuild.
Entire numerous families without any real modern means of transport were forced to leave their homes and native lands and move toward their lands of adoption. In fact temporary refugee camps were rapidly organized around the great urban conglomerations, and were considered the places that offered the best chances of survival.

As in every mass displacement of people it was not just poor families or depressed groups that were affected, but members of all castes and all social classes, men and women sometimes driven to seek a different future not just by the will to survive or by social and political opportunism, but also by idealism and principles. The government headed by India's new leader Jawaharlal Nehru was faced with an incredible emergency, having to cope with the reallocation and logistics required to handle such a huge influx of refugees and find ways of reintegrating the working population on a reasonable timescale and in a planned manner.
The protocol for new towns proposed by Koenigsberger seemed to offer a suitable solution precisely because new urban settlements would have been able to provide an immediate response to the urgent needs raised by a series of pressing questions: from the redistribution of wealth in the country to the reallocation of large numbers of people in a short space of time, while guaranteeing new social and hygienic

standards. The construction of these towns made it possible to develop a range of means for the building of the new democratic India, and among them the most useful seemed to be the modernization of methods of construction and production that would allow the standardization of processes and the promotion of new skills and new working activities.

For this reason projects already under way or processes already set in motion for the construction of modern towns were taken as a starting point and, on the basis of these, plans were made for the creation of hundreds of towns and cities scattered all over the country. [13] In general these were settlements that had a specific vocation and fostered a specific relationship between the new policies of the modern and democratic state, models of production and social and political hierarchies with respect to the territory. So we can speak of the conception of three programmatic types of city: the capital city, to decentralize power to the new territories marked out for the states of the Indian federation (which would include the well-known project for Chandigarh); industrial towns, created in poor and depressed areas to promote their accelerated development and the towns for refugees located on the margins of the historic cities, in particular along corridors linking interrelated areas of production.

So this readjustment, which left a deep mark on the country, was a venture of modern architecture and city planning that was highly concentrated in time, and the emergency, combined with the starkness of the situation, was the occasion for initiating and organizing one of the greatest territorial and urbanistic restructurings in the history of decolonization. It can be said in fact that modern city planning dragged independent India into the modern era by tackling, through a reflection on space, precise questions like representation of the new authority, the secularization of space and the social state, the values of the socialist and democratic state, modern industry as a means of adaptation to international standards and the social question as a practice of interreligious and interracial tolerance.

All this made possible an intellectual intention to create a different sensibility. The reinvention of modes of social and secular aggregation was associated with modern models of life based on the timescales of industry, the promotion and diffusion of standards of hygiene and sanitation and the minimal education of whole strata of the population. The new state bureaucracy, with the introduction of new institutional bodies, took on board the principles of the suffrage and representation of Indian citizens.

The projects for the federal capitals of Orissa and the Punjab, Bhubaneswar and Chandigarh, for the Tata Steel City, Jamshedpur, [14] for mining towns and for satellite towns of Delhi as well as Calcutta, Faridabad and Nilokheri, were part of a wide-ranging and far-reaching program [15] that was reaffirmed under the governments of Indira Gandhi and then her son Rajiv Gandhi, when isolated examples like the new capital of Gujarat, Gandhinagar, were realized.

Reconstructing this history through the study of three examples, chosen as a paradigm of the processes that have linked architecture to the development of the country, is of interest not just in order to understand what sort of political image and international scenario Nehru, an incredibly influential statesman of the postwar period, had set his sights on, but also to comprehend more in general the new horizons of contemporary architecture.

In fact India is currently viewed internationally as an emerging country with one of the most interesting models of development, and at the same time its architecture is attracting attention, while the unpredictable growth of its cities is posing some of the biggest questions in today's urban planning.

In contrast to those of other parts of the planet, urban agglomerations of spontaneous origin in India, if observed properly, show very strongly the effect of the legacy of the post-Partition approach to production. At the same time participatory and social architecture all over the world owes a debt to the "laboratory" of India through its protagonists who, after playing a part in the experiment, went all over the postcolonial world in the hope of initiating pacifying and transformative processes.

As has already been suggested, the main objectives set for the state program of development were a renewal of the system of administration and production to favor social mobility, an increase in literacy rates and levels of education to guarantee the involvement of the population in political decision making and determining the direction in which the country moved and finally a gradual opening up of the market in order to offer people the chance of a concrete personal emancipation. Thus it was possible to promote domestic economic growth through extensive state intervention while recognizing private and individual initiative as one of the principal engines of a widespread civil and technological development. This was the equivalent in domestic and day-to-day policy of the choices made in foreign policy, when the country opted for neutrality with respect to the positions of the two blocks of the Cold War, Soviet-style totalitarian communism and Anglo-American individualistic capitalism.

As emblematic cases of the dual nature of socialist and democratic India we can take two cities of contrasting nature and aspirations but which are simultaneously extremely consistent examples of the modern and systematic spirit as a whole: Bhubaneswar and Jamshedpur. At the same time we can utilize Faridabad as a paradigm of an adaption of that modern spirit to the complexity of the Indian situation.

A Feasible Modernity
–

In order to construct a fully modern city it was necessary to import skills and expertise from the West, and then adapt them to the local context, completely different from the technologically advanced one of Europe and the United States of America. Otto Koenigsberger, an architect and city planner who had fled from a Nazi and racist Germany, had arrived in India after a brief stay in Egypt to obtain a doctorate in archeology. Thus he was a person who had cultivated an appreciation of the history and cultural heritage of non-European contexts. His work in Jamshedpur and Bangalore made him the key man to oversee the Indian planning of new towns and cities. Which is why he was called on to draw up a protocol for bringing India into the modern era.

Planning is the salient characteristic and chief pleasure of people who form "groups" to attain an objective. This is the main reason why Koenigsberger was willing to participate in a plan that would include processes already under way and that, through these, would be able to assemble and unite different groups of people and systems of power and thus bring dissimilar orientations and goals together in a single, secular and tolerant vision. For this reason the planning of cities like Jamshedpur and Bhubaneswar, the former with a modern core already built, the second acclaimed as the new capital of Orissa after independence, was integrated into the protocol. · 16

In this sense the city was supposed to be constructed as a common platform, and secular space, intended as a version of European public space, would have made its appearance in India. At the same time and in a manner totally inseparable from the first, this was to bring about a drastic change in the Hindu and Moghul version of an immovable temporality, drawn out in India with the establishment of colonial rule.

In addition to this incredible upheaval in the way of conceiving the relationship between space and time, and only as a result of the need to bring into being places in which to root a new and drastically different vision of the world, the awareness of the necessity for a redistribution of wealth through space was confirmed. Public and secular space took the form of institutional centers of representation, small and large institutes with responsibility for sanitation and health, theaters and movie houses, kindergartens, schools and universities as well as open parks and playgrounds for children and young people, markets, stores, office buildings and transport infrastructure. Principles that are typical of the choices of a democratic and social policy. And protocols for planning the social impact of the change were also being brought into play. Protocols of education in the use and understanding of the new management of public space and authority. The way was paved for the establishment of processes of participation in the initiatives, means were devised for the promotion of self-help and the foundations were laid for the institution of the current microcredit system. It is important to reflect on this aspect, however controversial the principle of encouraging indebtedness in the most desperately impoverished classes and social groups may be.

Lastly, two equally fundamental questions for the identity of a modern and democratic government came to the fore in the drawing up of the protocol: the form that the representation of demo-cratic rule and Indian sovereignty should take and the adaptation of industrial technology to social capacities and local needs. On the one hand, therefore, an elegant and cultivated version of modern architecture was produced, and on the other a series of studies were launched into the modification of building and prefabrication technology to suit the geographical and climatic context. The results of this pioneering research would be codified into a set of norms and a specific grammar that is commonly classified under the label of tropical architecture. · 17 The whole range of necessary changes was undertaken in a natural way, and with a spontaneity and energy that came from a faith in an enlightened vision and in progressive science, with a full acceptance of the wretched state of the reality that had to be dealt with. The decided rejection of the status quo in the country was, in any case, made necessary by the abrupt change of course and by the international climate.

Their conception was made possible through the interpenetration and development of advanced Western models, and so it was considered necessary to import knowhow, instruments, spatial systems, technology and machinery, as well as to involve architects and city planners in the research, so that they could organize processes of adaptation and training of local workers and groups.

The Paradigm
–

In a first phase, thanks to the expertise of Otto Koenigsberger, the objectives of the New Towns Protocol were laid out, outlining the specific vocations of the new urban settlements, and as a consequence the locations and distribution of the cities and towns to be founded. Subsequently, through a convergence of reflections on the urban question, a paradigm was defined that could be adapted to different urban functions: the band town pattern.

Right from its name, the urban project drawn up by Koenigsberger appears to be an anomaly: in fact it is not an ideal plan of a city or a social utopia, but a scheme/sample, conceived as if it were the pattern of an "urban fabric." Later it would be adapted to the context; the form, dimensions and composition of its parts would be marked out on the basis of the figure, i.e. landscape, to which it had to adapt. What mattered, therefore, was its quality, its resistance, its fiber, the subtle interweaving of its components, its softness and elasticity. And in the urban fabric this is linked to the inseparable relationship that is created between the built and the builder, between the planner and the inhabitant, between the person who represents and the person who is represented. So the band town pattern is an urban landscape composed of design, materials and the people who live in it: in short it is a concept that can be adapted to any context. Further on three primary versions of the band town pattern will be analyzed: a capital city (Bhubaneswar, in Orissa), an industrial one (Jamshedpur in Jharkhand) and a city for refugees (Faridabad in the Delhi region).

The new urban landscape developed under the guidance of Otto Koenigsberger was revolutionary but derived in many aspects from a reworking of the theories on the garden city and those on the modern city of the Siedlungen, both in its architectural and urban grammar, which still reflected the pleasure taken in an aesthetics of language, and in the ideal tendency of a socialist character that permeated its principal guidelines.

The Protocol
—

The idea of importing from Europe the most up-to-date technologies for the processing of iron ore and the production of steel and linking them to a social development integrated with works and services and associated with a low-density urban environment had been put into effect at Jamshedpur between 1911 and 1936, but it was only with the launch of the New Towns Protocol that the small industrial town acquired the full status of a city. The project for Jamshedpur was the starting point and thus became the pilot project for the foundation of new towns. The "band town" was laid out around a central artery intended for vehicular traffic and to provide a connection with the surrounding region. Secondary roads branched off it on each side; through these the urbanized territory would be permeated by all the infrastructures required for the configuration of an urban fabric. This means that the band town pattern had been conceived as a land-use plan, an

intelligent design of proportional relationships that would mold the territory to its uses through their disposition and allow places to be open to permeation by social life. In fact Koenigsberger combined the idea of the precise design of the ground (usually considering a section extending from -3m to +3m, i.e. one containing both the water and sewage system and the electricity grid) with that of an equally carefully planned and complex composition of the neighborhood unit. The neighborhood unit was in fact conceived as a social mechanism and a means of guaranteeing the introduction of the principles of the new popular participation in the government of the country. Thus a tight linkage of the rights and duties of the inhabitants, all too bureaucratic and hierarchical, made it possible to determine the location and value of the housing to which families would have access on the basis of their position within the productive, social and finally political community. This position would give them the right to a greater or lesser proximity to services, stores, bus and railroad stations, the airport, entrances to highways and workplaces; in short their entire mobility and their access to social relations was controlled by a precise organization based on the design of architecture. This kind of all too trusting attitude toward architectural design, even if dated, is one that might well be adopted again today, now that architecture is losing the right to be beautiful and designed, in virtue of an occasional value of temporary utility, given that, as we are well aware, it is created to last while its use varies according to the needs of the context. It should be said moreover that the idea of outlining a paradigm owes a great deal to early modern reflections on the city and its form. In fact elements pertaining to cultures of design that are very remote from one another are mixed up in the plan. [18] In it we can find first of all the infrastructural advantages offered by the linear city, a vision originally put forward by an engineer, Soria y Mata, but taken up again in Stalingrad after the war in a version adapted to the local context. In the case of the Indian cities, however, it was given a totally different form and drawn out in time: for example, road infrastructure was to be constructed according to a precise hierarchical plan that identified at least "seven types" to be realized in stages, first in dirt, then in cement, and only subsequently with an asphalt or cement surface. The program is also profoundly indebted to the guidelines laid down in Ebenezer Howard's designs for the Garden City. Through the low residential density of detached houses linked together by services and the tertiary sector, the aim was on the one hand to reduce the steadily growing congestion in the big cities, and on the other to integrate the countryside and provide the environmental advantages of a direct connection with the land. In India this seemed an ideal way of responding to a different set of conditions. First of all the population was accustomed to living in the open air and its extended families were used to sharing domestic spaces. And then the rural and backward conditions of the society in general raised questions about the type of modernization possible in the country. Two different currents emerged in political debate with regard to this last point. One supported the hypothesis of an agrarian modernization, maintaining a close relationship with the countryside and a practice of subsistence farming that made reference to the precepts and figure of Gandhi; [19] the other was linked to a model of rapid industrialization in accordance with the theories of economic development of the time and looked instead to Nehru for support. [20] In short to outline a modern urban paradigm that could reconcile industrial production and agricultural production it would be necessary to dilute and mix the opposite positions on the future of the India taken by the two founding fathers of the country. Another extremely interesting link between this debate and the European one on the modern city is the clear reference to the paradigm of the band town, to the idea of a semi-industrial city conceived by Tessenow for Karl Schmidt at Hellerau, in Germany. In fact for Tessenow at that moment the city provided the pretext for a reflection on the secular space linked to the new industrial technology. Two of Tessenow's insights are still extremely relevant, the first on tolerance, the second on technology.

The need to find a conceptual basis for the integration of the short timescale of human life and the long one of industrial machinery in urban space was clear. He came up with a remarkable solution, deciding that the harmonious rhythm of movement in space was what living beings and inanimate objects had in common. And so he placed a new kind of theater at the institutional heart of the city: the Festspielhaus, birthplace of eurhythmics, other-

wise known as the Dalcroze Method. Thus an individual and collective choice of coexistence through conscious cooperation resulted in a slight decentralization of the symbolic role of industry (in that case, the client), government and politics (at a time of radical ideological clashes) and, last but far from least, the religious institutions: it is well known that anti-Semitism, racism and xenophobia on a confessional basis were growing stronger in the Germany of those days, and they were to became a crude and merciless reality in 1933. In India after Partition and right up to the present day the question of the possibility of using space to build tolerance is a very real one and a new prospect for a version of secular space linked to the time of its uses seems to have been opened up in Rahul Mehrotra's concept of the Kinetic City. [21]

At the same time Tessenow had hypothesized the realization of a range of prefabricated structures for Hellerau, in particular a light wall with a wooden framework that would have made it easier to construct housing, stimulated the training of specialized workers and made possible, if necessary, the customization of elements. All aspects that in the India of that time proved fundamental to the establishment of a new building industry, the organization of urban areas that could be predetermined and rapidly assembled and the differentiation of the final elements in situ. And aspects that are still fundamental to the integration of the skills traditionally developed and handed down within extended families and that show in fact how mass production is not nowadays exclusively done by machinery in industrial complexes: the manufacturing compounds of slums like Dharavi are organized more on the basis of one person duplicating items at a time.

Lastly, I would also like to look at the link with the functionalist city as it was conceived by an idealist like Ernst May on the outskirts of Frankfurt, [22] when, following the construction of the Weissenhof Estate, he designed residential districts on the basis of new codes related to a new quality of life, with detached houses set side by side, row houses and blocks of apartments, with the aim of bringing different social classes together and encouraging a mixed use of the city. In fact commercial zones were planned at the ends of the districts as locations for small local stores, libraries, post offices and institutional services, and above all to provide access to the railroads or rapid surface transit systems. And so even today, instead of gated communities, dormitory suburbs and office districts, we could think about urban zones with a complex use for a city open to daily life.

This last point is closely connected with the final element introduced in India through the New Towns Protocol, the idea of the neighborhood unit. The concept, developed by Clarence Perry in 1929 as a basis for expansion of the city, hinged on six fundamental points: size, boundaries, open spaces, spaces for services, local shopping areas and an internal system of streets. It should not be forgotten that the studies of Patrick Geddes had fostered in India the idea of planning as a great game played out between inhabitants and planners, to be activated on the level of the city. The neighborhood unit was chosen by Koenigsberger as the ideal place in which bring about a full correspondence between action and educational spiral, i.e. the territory in which the citizen learns the rules of democratic life through cooperation.

The Legacy
–

Finally, there was nothing naïve about the desire to intertwine Western capacities, know-how and technology in a paradigmatic synthesis. On the contrary, it was a practical way of bringing experts into close contact with young local professionals and workers and training them in new skills. It should be remembered, in fact, that a large number of Indians were involved in the Protocol for New Towns, some of whom had important positions and managerial roles, like P.L. Varma and Julius Vaz. In the main construction projects, moreover, those of Jamshedpur and Chandigarh, [23] young Indian architects were involved, not just as trainees but also as foremen, works supervisors, intermediaries and experts on local techniques and practices. Their association with figures of the caliber of Matthew Nowicki, Albert Mayer, Pierre Jeanneret, Charlotte Perriand, Jane Drew and Maxwell Fry allowed them not only to develop their own version of modern architecture, as did Balkrishna V. Doshi, A.G. Krishna Menon, Charles Correa and Raj Rewal to mention just the best known, but also and above all to put modern technology to the test and grasp its limits

and potential. The result was a new and noble approach to the handling of its components, with regard both to its adaptation to the local context and to its stylistic integration: in short a new alchemy was defined in the relationship between space, architecture and climate. An alchemy that was not confined to architecture but found expression in a sensitive and delicate way of inserting new urban settlements into the landscape. Today we would describe such a sensitivity as environmental for the manner in which it sought to foster the coexistence of human and natural ecosystems through the study and integration of an architecture that would be intelligent and balanced in its use of land, resources, technology and components. [24]

So what was referred to as "importing modernity" was an expedient to reduce the huge gap that was opening up between self-ruled countries and colonies, between centers and peripheries, between urban settlements and spontaneous ones.

But it should be remembered that in other parts of the world modernity was synonymous with a second colonization, with the mechanical stripping of resources and the institutionalization of gated communities, resulting in an increase in segregation and even taken to the extreme of apartheid. So there is an important question to be asked in order to reorient a possible future: what is modernity? Or to put it another way, what kind of modernity makes possible a democratic and libertarian spirit? In fact science does not bring awareness in itself. It is its use, its connection with life, its involvement in people's actions and their integration with nature that produce an ethics of hope. And in that period the idea of nurturing hope in an improvement of society stemmed precisely from the new experiences and the new needs for the construction of a possible modernity, a negotiated modernity.

Perspectives
–

The Indian paradigm opens up a perspective of reflection on this aspect. After the Indian case, that way of thinking spread, and produced a new awareness of democracy in the relationship between peoples and territories, in the reciprocal relationship between wealth and redistribution. As Giordano Bruno said to Sagredo: "humanity has conceived the seed of utopia and gestation is proceeding toward its inevitable birth."

From the Indian paradigm followed a series of fundamental questions, in the first place the idea, widely accepted in our own day, that there is an aesthetics of process: an aesthetics so evident that it eclipses questions of style, language and grammar, in the urban as well as the architectural sphere.

The fact remains that the best exponents of the modern participatory paradigm are those who include traditional aesthetic aspects among the objectives of the process. C. Correa and B.V. Doshi, for example, have come up with the principle of incremental architecture, including growth in a logic of planning that provides for the exceptionality of its final form. The same idea lies at the base of Aravena's architecture, to cite the winner of the Prizker Prize in 2016 and curator of the 15th Biennale di Venezia. [25] But the course of the contemporary architecture that owes a debt to modernity is not just one that turns back on itself, wrapping itself up in codes and quotations, however magnificent they may appear even in my eyes and however much they have the ring of pure poetry. [26] The course of modern architecture has been richer and more varied and has produced in its more pragmatic version other codes that are equally full of meaning, of new and different forms of poetry.

From the aesthetic characterization of processes are in fact germinating new prospects for contemporary architecture, and not exclusively in its pauperist or marginal aspect. Rather the one that is descended from a great history of shared architecture, as projects were once always shared between architects and clients, between patrons and artists. So it is normal that a new, and ever more conscious link should be emerging today between citizens, representation, planners and architects.

NOTES

[1]
H. Lefebvre, *Le Droit à la ville* (Paris: Anthropos, 1968).

[2]
G. Bachelard, *The New Scientific Spirit* (Boston: Beacon Press, 1985).

[3]
G. Ferraro, *Rieducazione alla Speranza* (Milan: Jaca Book, 1988). P. Geddes, *Cities in Evolution* (London: Williams & Norgate, 1915).

[4]
The correct spelling of the name is Königsberger, but as a result of him spending much of his life in English-speaking countries it is usually transcribed as Koenigsberger.

[5]
V. Baweja, *A Pre-history of Green Architecture: Otto Koenigsberger and Tropical Architecture, from Princely Mysore to Post-colonial London*, PhD thesis, University of Michigan, 2008. Available online at http://deepblue.lib.umich.edu/handle/2027.42/60709.

[6]
R.R. Mehrotra, A.J. Agarwal and S. Ganguly, *Nehru: Man among Men* (New Delhi: R.H Mital, 1990).

[7]
R. Riboldazzi, *La costruzione della città moderna* (Milan: Jaca Books, 2010). R. Riboldazzi, *Un'altra modernità: L'IFHTP e la cultura urbanistica tra le due guerre, 1923-1939* (Rome: Gangemi, 2009).

[8]
By the term Protocol for the New Town of Modern Foundation is meant the set of small and medium-sized towns whose location and construction were decided on during the political reorganization of India under the first Nehru government in order to redistribute wealth and define modern standards of living. Given the difficulties encountered in the negotiations over the founding of each of them, there is no single document but a series of them, even though the standards and processes are identical and all based on the indications of O. Koenigsberger and the band town paradigm. As a consequence thereference to a Protocol for the New Town of Modern Foundation has entered into common use. O. Koenigsberger, "New Towns in India," *Town Planning Review*, no. 23 (1925).

[9]
G. Zucconi, *La città contesa* (Milan: Jaca Book, 1989).

[10]
R. Khalia, "Modernism, Modernization and Post-colonial India: A Reflective Essay," *Planning Perspectives*, no. 21 (April 2006), 133-56.

[11]
R. Mehrotra, *Architecture in India since 1990* (Mumbai: Pictor Publishing, 2011).

[12]
D. Ponzini and M. Nastasi, *Starchitecture* (Turin: Umberto Allemandi, 2011).

[13]
B. Ghosh, "New Towns in India: A Home, a Cow, an Acre of Land," *Lotus International*, no. 34 (1982), 18-31.

[14]
R. Lee, "Constructing a Shared Vision: Otto Koenigsberger and Tata & Sons," *ABE Journal* (2012), http://dev.abejournal.eu/index.php?id=356.

[15]
O. Koenigsberger, "New Towns in India," *Town Planning Review*, no. 23 (1925).

[16]
R. Kalhia, *Bhubaneswar: From a Temple Town to a Capital City* (Carbondale: Southern Illinois University Press, 1994).

[17]
O. Koenigsberger, T.G. Ingersoll, A. Mayhew and S.V. Szokolay, *Manual of Tropical Housing and Building* (London: Longman, 1974).

[18]
L. Benevolo, *Le origini dell'urbanistica moderna* (Bari: Laterza, 1991).

[19]
R. Khosla, "Indian Rural Architecture," *Lotus International*, no. 34 (1982), 84-90.

[20]
Independence and After: A Collection of the More Important Speeches of Jawaharlal Nehru from September 1946 to May 1949 (Delhi: The Publications Division, Government of India, 1950).

[21]
R. Mehrotra, *Mapping Mumbai* (Mumbai: Mumbai Design Research Institute, 2006).

[22]
D.W. Dreysse, *May-Siedlungen. Architekturfuerer durch acht Siedlungen des Neue Frankfurt, 1923-1930*, (Cologne: Walther König, 1994). Ernst May was city architect and planner in Frankfurt from 1925 to 1930.

[23]
H-U. Khan, J. Beinart and C. Correa (eds.), *Le Corbusier: Chandigarh and the Modern City* (Ahmedabad: Mapin Publishing, 2009).

[24]
B. Albrecht, *Conservare il Futuro. Il pensiero della sostenibilità in architettura* (Padua: Il Poligrafo, 2012).

[25]
A. Aravena and A. Iacobelli, *Elemental: Incremental Housing and Participatory Design Manual* (Ostfildern: Hatje Cantz, 2013). http://www.elementalchile.cl. Aravena won the Silver Lion at the 2008 Venice Biennale with his project Elemental.

[26]
M. D'Alfonso, "The Urgency of the Future", in B. Albrecht (ed.), *Africa, Big Change, Big Chance* ß(Milan: Compositori, 2014).

ESTABLISHING AN ARCHITECTURAL IDENTITY IN AN AGE OF GLOBALIZATION

/

PAOLO BRESCIA

The Information Age, characterized by the evolution of technology to a point where it is an indispensible part of daily life even in the most far-flung corners of the globe, has resulted in the creation of a knowledge based society, where ideas and information are exchanged at the speed of light and global communications and networking constantly shape modern society.

The resultant high-tech global economy has given impetus to wide-ranging trans-national economic, social and cultural changes in recent years. In this context, emerge some questions about the role of architecture. Has architecture, which was once specific and local, become interchangeable and global? Is architecture still rooted in national identity, or has it been sacrificed on the altar of globalization? If architecture is the physical embodiment of socio-cultural aspirations, what form should it take to remain relevant in a rapidly mutating world?

The meetings of CIAM, Team X, Metabolism and Any regularly led architects to discuss conditions of architecture in relation to general culture, to modernity, to globalization, taking note of an increasingly fluctuating and indeterminate reality as opposed to the Vitruvian triad of *firmitas, utilitas and venustas* and leading to a shared view that the traditional concept of architecture understood as something necessarily entrenched in a site, should be reconsidered. In the 20th century these debates led to the rise of architectural movements such as Modernism, which focused on the purity of form and function and the honest expression of structure

and materials as a progressive "modern" approach, in reaction to the lavish stylistic excesses, which characterized the architecture of the previous eras.

In the Western world fuelled by the need to re-invent and on occasion even erase, battle-scarred national identities after the World Wars, the simplification of architecture to a purist aesthetic was the result of both a practical requirement to re-build and cater to the demands of rapidly changing economies fuelled by industrialization, and a socio-political expression of the democratization of society.

Interestingly enough, the parallel political upheavals that resulted in the dissolution of colonialism in many parts of the non-Western world also led to the development of a fertile new ground for the introduction of Modernist architecture as a means to "modernization", to create a forward-thinking, anti-colonialist identity for newly liberated nations. However, as this book also attempts to establish, in countries such as India with its intrinsic unique culture that has spanned several millennia, it quickly became evident to the Western pioneers of Modernism that their architecture could not exist as an alien import that is merely trans-located. Instead, there was a strong need to assimilate with the age-old, socio-cultural framework and the diametrically opposite political philosophies of youthful idealism that characterized the newly liberated nation. Thus, in a society replete with strong cultural traditions characterized by a philosophy of tolerance and limited by current financial resources, the rational industrial approach that characterized Modernism was itself transformed both through physical and economic circumstances as well as the organic necessity to adapt and to root itself within the national psyche if it was to grow, flourish and thrive. Within this international debate, the Italian case presents some specifics that could be examined through the phenomenon that Pierluigi Nicolin had defined as contextualism and internationalism of Italian architecture.

As it happens for other cases of intellectual emigration, for Italian architects too, work abroad presented the platform for testing their own identity in the design response to the diversity of contexts. An experience similar to that of the pioneering Western Modernists as they struggled to establish their voice in non-Western nations such as India, within an entirely new social, cultural, geographic, climatic and economic context that challenged their preconceptions in an entirely different way.

At the same time on the international stage there was a change of paradigm: thinkers from the Frankfurt School, nihilistics or hermeneutics such as Blumenberg, Starobinski, Vattimo, Severino, Deleuze, Derrida, information theorists such as Eco, Baudrillard, Virilio, and behaviorists as Augé, Urry, Lash, Sennett, Inghilleri, have started a new thought on urban and social dynamics, considering them specific to the present situation.

It is in this context that a new urban and social consciousness has developed on the part of the younger generation, who are more interested in the kind of action-reaction processes within the body of the city. This approach extends the vision beyond the physical boundaries of architecture and at the same time limits the scope of predetermined actions. It takes note of the failures of urbanism and big plans (un-programmable, by definition) and gives birth to interest in the intermediate scale: that of urban design.

But how to frame this young generations attitude within the structure of contemporary globalization? If for globalization we intend the planetary ensemble of the means of circulation and of the network of communication, then a key of interpretation may be provided from the juxtaposition that Paul Virilio identifies through world-city and city-world. The world has become a world-city, within which products of all types circulate and exchange, including messages, images, fashions, artists... architects. But it is also true that the city is a world-city, with its ethnic, cultural and social differences. In this sense, the city-world belies the illusions of the world-city. It is on this uncertain terrain, suspended between the city and the world, where we think architects are called to act today.

The phenomenon that we are seeing in recent years is a sort of awareness of local identity, quite different from the previous industrial age, where many emerging economies rejected traditional and regional metaphors perceived as an antithesis to their modern and democratic aspirations. Instead, perhaps as a result of the resurgent individualism, which the technological age facilitates, emerging markets in Asia and Africa are looking for ways to re-establish and retain their increasingly fragile national identities, as they are now more conscious of establishing their place in the global arena. In this new global scenario, also the international urban marketing has chosen to focus more on the logic of differentiation and uniqueness starting from the cultural and social identities of the specific promoter (public or private).

So the issue is: how can Architecture remain relevant in this changing scenario, where on one hand we are witnessing the rise of neo-colonialists—the all-pervasive, multi-national brands, some of which even more economically powerful than several nations, that are determined to install their identity on a global platform,—and on the other we have the intrinsic human need for recognition, for individual expression, within the increasingly cross-cultural, amorphous global milieu?

Another interesting phenomenon that the Technological Age unlocks is the ease of customization. Computerized technologies, which allow customers to pick and choose from a kit of parts and interpretively develop mass-produced consumer goods to reflect their individuality, empower designers with a never-ending palette of possibilities, thereby creating a new economically and efficient bespoke aesthetic, which can be accessible to all. Further advancements such as 3D printing indicate that this is just the beginning of the phenomenon of individualization.

In our experience, the use of similar technology utilized in less industrialized economies such as India, which still retain an affordable, thriving, traditional arts and crafts culture, can also empower architects and artisans to cooperate in new and interesting ways. In one of our recent design experience merging parametric algorithmic design in combination with basic artisan construction techniques, it was possible to develop a real estate project with both social and environmental sustainability, translating into the valorization of local art and craft workers, thereby contributing to the local economic and cultural development of the region. Thus, it was possible to use technology to delineate in a contemporary way ancient motifs of material culture, which are by now well-established in the collective imagination, allowing also for a participatory architecture, where the artisans are able to identify their contribution in the larger development. This approach recalls the concept of multiplicity, based on repetition where individuals can find their own identity (craftsmanship/ customization), rather than on multiplication (industrial mass-production/ replication).

Parallel to this, is our present experience in Ghana, where lack of a traditional urban memory of an ambitious large scale development has in reality enabled the opportunity for the creation of new public spaces. This research does not merely evolve from a stand-alone functional program, but as a consequence of behavioral situations in local community life (in this case referring to the typical compound house of equatorial Africa), through which it will be possible to create an urban effect through the contemporary reinterpretation of an aggregative traditional model. As in a stage setting, public life is visually evoked, rather than physically built, with the aim to catalyze the impulse to a greater social involvement. This experience has allowed us to go beyond the classic opposition public/private, individual/society, architecture/environment, towards a new dimension of "common good" understood as social and psychological capital, as a place shared by all the members of the community. In this sense, the goal is not a project *for* Ghana, but *by* Ghana.

In the light of these experiences, we are increasingly converging on the idea of design understood as the outcome (rather than the initialization) of a cooperative evolutionary process. Architecture is not an individual matter, but a common task that will reveal within globalization the awareness of individual identities and cultural specificities, which will be much more valued, as intense international exchanges which are fundamental for the future.

Moreover, architecture, so anchored to its own site, must dependent on others and more dynamic means to spread the ideas it produces. To spread ideas is necessary to give them life and to test them in the world.

urban tropical landscape

PHOTO BY MARCO INTROINI

Marco Introini's artistic vision makes it possible to discern a new code in architecture and in the design of the urban landscape. The new tropical architecture was developed to adapt modernity to a luxuriant natural setting and mitigate the rigors of an inhospitable climate, while establishing new standards and finding new means of formulating conventions of participation and cooperation.

The warmth of this landscape of tropical modernity was to become part of the collective imagination. It was the first step in the creation of a democratic and transnational version of modernity that has spread through the marginal regions on the periphery of the world.

WARM MODERNITY

WARM MODERNITY

C

MODERNITY
AS A TOOL

Interpretative filters

/

RESEARCH BY MADDALENA D'ALFONSO

Parameters that integrate processes of activation of societies into spatial qualities.

1.
SECULARIZATION AND THE CONSEQUENT SOCIAL IMPACT
/

The process by which sociopolitical institutions and cultural life are rendered progressively independent of the control and influence of religion and the Church makes secularization one of the salient features of modernity. Architectural and urban plans provide for the construction of public space that can be adapted to any use. Tolerance in space is possible in the absence of identifying symbols. The possibility of a temporary characterization of places permits coexistence.

2.
DEMOCRACY AND THE REPRESENTATION OF POWER
/

The ideal result of democratization is to guarantee that people have the right to vote and that everyone receives the same safeguards and can play an active part in the political system.
In architecture this aspect signifies implementation of rights through space, and thus places where these rights can be recognized and exercised. From this follows the importance of a linguistic and grammatical adaptation to local contexts.

3.
INDUSTRIALIZATION AND THE IMPACT OF TECHNOLOGY
/

By this is meant a process of transformation of a society from a rural stage of subsistence farming to an industrial one, with a marked urban migration and abandonment of the countryside for work in factories. The effects of this on the landscape are visible on a territorial scale, in terms not just of the infrastructure required for the organization of industrial complexes but also, given the magnitude of their production, of the logistics for supply of the systems and for distribution of goods.

4.
TIME AND FEASIBILITY
/

The human perception of time and the social organization of time are important factors. The perception of time, in fact, undergoes significant changes in modernity. People discover new possibilities for the organization of their daily lives and identify new ritual moments in the course of their lives and their social interactions.
In architecture new spatial and urban systems emerge, such as the ones devoted to leisure and entertainment during time free from work.

AN INDUTRIAL CITY
JAMSHEDPUR

/

MADDALENA D'ALFONSO

Planned population: 200 000
1944-45 plan by Otto Koenigsberger

–

Jamshedpur was the pilot project of the entire protocol for new Indian towns drawn up after independence. It was founded with the idea of creating a large manufacturing community, the fruit of an agreement between the Indian state and the Tata Iron and Steel Company Ltd, to serve as the country's main center for the production of steel. The modern urban nucleus was built prior to the launch of the Nehru-Koenigsberger protocol, but the coherent planning of a logical and efficient layout was entrusted to O. Koenigsberger as the first real attempt to build a modern settlement in India. It was on this first occasion that Koenigsberger outlined the model of the band town, in which the fusion of the British practices of planning developed by Ebenezer Howard and German ones is evident both in the organization of the settlement's structure around the neighborhood unit and in the character of the designs for the commercial and business center and for the models of housing.

The scheme bears witness to the eclectic genealogy of planning in India. It was drawn up for the location of the new headquarters of the Tata steelworks in one of India's poorest regions and, at the same, as a response to the urgent need to relieve the pressure on the country's historic and colonial urban centers. The plan set out to create a clear separation between industrial and residential areas, and to facilitate the horizontal development of means of transport by rail and road, with the aim of reducing the level of investment in infrastructure but ensuring the free movement of people and goods. Paying direct attention to the design of the land for the first time, the band town model indicated a new system for its division into lots that optimized facilities and structures, with the objective of obviating a priori the effects of rapid and unchecked overpopulation, a common problem in centers of industrial production.

The urban prototype that stemmed from this was that of a low-density city which would develop horizontally and was subdivided into functional sectors and autonomous neighborhood units laid out along a single main traffic artery. Each unit in Jamshedpur was made up of around 15 000 people, a much higher number than in the Western models of reference. An unsettling aspect was the introduction of new techniques for the construction of housing, owing both to their typologies and to the involvement of a new and more advanced building industry that was beginning to make use of prefabricated elements. In this way the protocol was linked with the promotion of skills and capacities in the communities involved, with the aim of training new and specialized workers able to construct buildings that adhered to standardized hygienic and sanitary principles and to do so at speed. The solutions adopted had to be suited to the tropical Indian climate and local modes of habitation. It was with this experience that Koenigsberger sowed the seeds for research into tropical architecture, prompting a great development of ideas and techniques in India and in the rest of the world.

The plan ushered in a programmatic model of the town that can be defined as an "urban paradigm" since it forged, for the first time, an inseparable link between modern aesthetics and a process of introduction of new ethical values in underdeveloped countries: the urban objective sprang from the desire to turn the archaic nuclei and ties of rural communities into new and dynamic social structures organized on an urban basis. Thus the Indian urban paradigm took account of the desire for self-determination in the Indian society of the time and of the political choice to move toward a secular and democratic organization of socialist inspiration.

Some of the ideas that went into this new design, which inextricably bound together a set of ethical principles and modern aesthetics in a spatial configuration can be traced back to the work of Patrick Geddes in India: the preface of the report on the Jamshedpur Development Plan explicitly cites the text "Valley Section and Social Diagnostic" as a guide. In support of this processual and pluralistic idea aimed at introducing a disciplined social organization into modern urban nuclei scattered around the territory, the hope is expressed in the report on the Jamshedpur plan that, instead of relying on laws and regulations, the character of the city's image might be entrusted to an artist in order to guarantee its attractiveness and lack of uniformity. This would be preferable to leaving the choice in private hands, which would run the risk of an emphasis on saving money and a resulting homogenization of the urban space.

The formulation of this principle triggered the singular phenomenon that, in the discipline of architecture, has in fact favored a virtuoso and pluralistic process—even when demagogic—in the planning of new popular and social urban areas. In contrast the search for a language and grammar of modern architecture that would be able to embrace a new vision of social coexistence and the redistribution of rights and duties that ought to characterize the new democratic states slowly lost its centrality.

modern times

JAMSH

ANNA NURRA

EDPUR

As the band town pattern was a conceptual paradigm it could be adapted to the site and the topography of the region: the Subarnarekha River formed a natural barrier to the growth of the city to the north and west; the troughs of the catchment basin, alternating with woodland and the beds of seasonal watercourses, shaped a diverse terrain. A railroad line connected the city with Calcutta and the capital Delhi.

Jamshedpur was divided up into functional sectors, with industry in the south and housing in the north, and the presence of the first low-density residential nucleus constituted an original element.
The planned population was 200 000, and the criterion established for the size of each unit was the distance that could be traversed on foot by children to reach their schools. The city is made up of sixteen neighborhood units organized around a winding traffic artery. Inserted between the troughs in the ground, they benefited from a natural ventilation and exploited the slope for the discharge of rainwater during the monsoon. The neighborhood units varied on the basis of the topography, and were integrated with the original nucleus. They housed between 10 000 and 18 000 people, with the number of houses ranging from 2000 to 3500, and covered an area of around 100 hectares. Each unit had its own civic center: a public space with buildings for services and leisure facilities.

The design of the residential areas and the open space is very complex and varied, creating a sophisticated ecological network between the parks of the city, the banks of the seasonal rivers, woodlands and pastures and the banks of the Subarnarekha.

1.
SECULARIZATION
AND ITS SOCIAL IMPACT
/

PUBLIC SPACES, available, accessible, open and planted with vegetation, formed the basis of the plan: places with no religious, social or ethnic connotations in order to attenuate social hierarchies that were characterized by segregation and radical conflict.

The civic center was the beating heart of the neighborhood unit: an area with a post office, outpatient clinic, market and spaces for recreation, and thus linked to everyday activities. It was here that the community services were provided, along with the means for the participation of residents in the administration and life of the city. It was regarded too as the location for exchanges of a two-way nature, not just of material goods but also of ideas.

The form of the houses, suited to the tropical climate and Indian lifestyle, made possible a continuity between public and semipublic space. The band town pattern was a complex plan of land use that provided for the coexistence of large public, semipublic and private open spaces. Thus it was the basis for the creation of a place where it would be possible to construct a community and a participatory society.

DWELLINGS		BANKS RIVERS	
BUSINESS CENTER		PLAY GROUND	
INDUSTRY		CIVIC CENTER	
RAPPRESENTATIVE CENTERS		AIRPORT	
ROADS		WATERBODIES	
RAILWAY		BYPASS	

800m

2.
DEMOCRACY AND THE REPRESENTATION
OF POWER
/

THE PARADIGM FOR A DEMOCRATIC city was the promotion of new collective values and new social rights: in the first place that of health care. Each district was equipped with an outpatient clinic, allowing even the poorest section of the community to make use of the primary services. The neighborhood unit contained an element of social diversity, in which the hierarchy was based on proximity to the civic center and the size of the house and its open space. Each unit had two primary schools and one middle school, located in the playgrounds, with the aim of promoting integration from an early age.

Indian democracy adopted a modern aesthetic. The design of the business center recalls the rationalist buildings of Gropius: a comb structure on the street front with six glass towers of 12 stories and a base with commercial activities. The architecture of the houses is reminiscent of the aesthetics of the German Siedlungen: pure and simple volumes whose bare plastered walls were patterned by a system of slightly projecting brise soleil, mostly located above the windows.

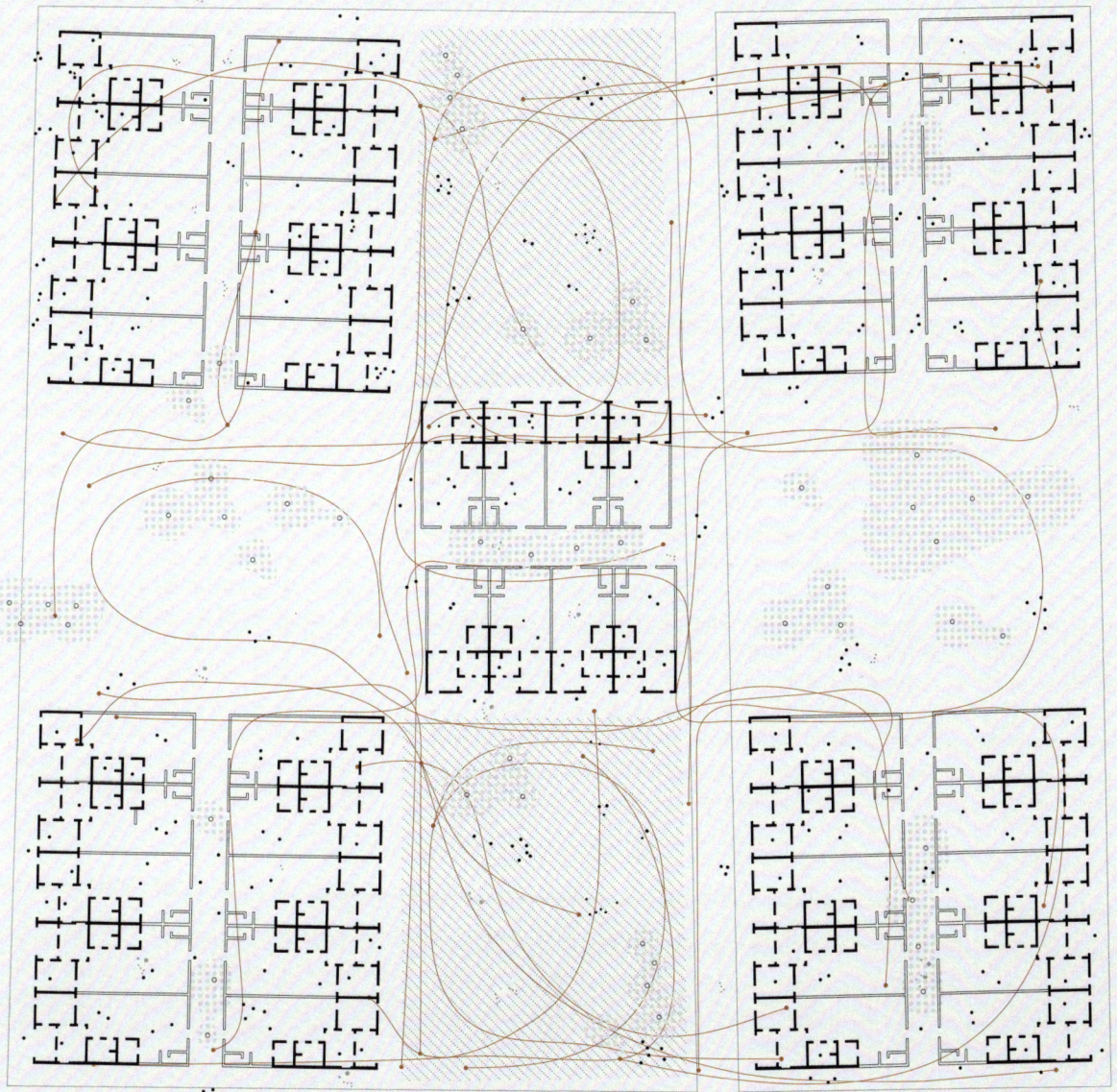

PLAN

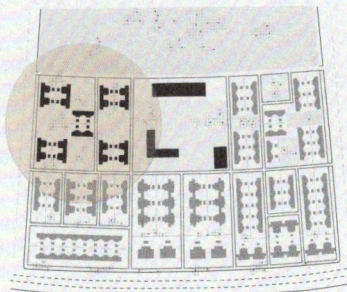

●━━━●	FLUXES
∷∷∷∷	TREE
███	DWELLINGS
·	PEOPLE
○	COWS
	CAMELS

0m   10m   20m

Indian Architecture Building Democracy

3.
INDUSTRIALIZATION AND THE IMPACT OF TECHNOLOGY
/

NEW TECHNIQUES RELYING on prefabrication were adapted to the tropical context to make it possible to carry out the process of modernization within a short period of time. A series of standards were introduced and applied to housing, roads and the water supply and sewage system. Tata itself contributed to the production of prefabricated elements: in fact an industrialization of building was necessary to ensure development.

Each dwelling consisted of a veranda and a number of rectangular prefabricated units that could be assembled in different ways in order to vary the form and dimensions of the house. The kitchen and bathroom faced onto the internal garden.
Modernist technology was combined with local techniques and simple stratagems to increase the level of comfort: keeping the house in contact with the ground permitted the dissipation of heat, an enclosure sheltered it from hot winds and dust, the internal openings provided adequate illumination and ventilation and the screening offered protection against exposure to the sun. Local workers were employed in the construction process, through precise training programs.

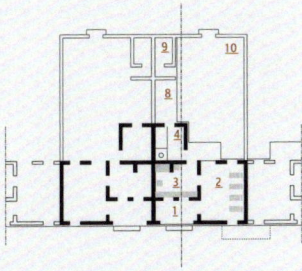

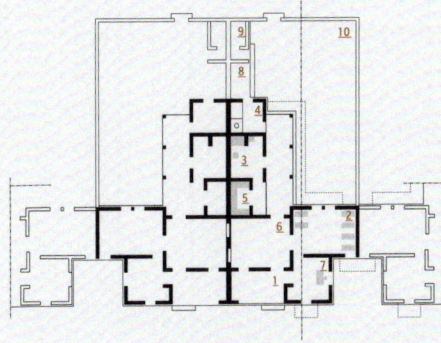

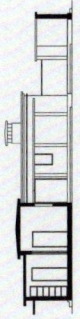

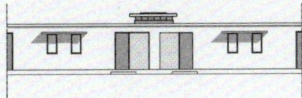

LIVING AREA: 24 MQ
PLINTH AREA: 32 MQ
VAIN: 4
PEOPLE: 2 /4

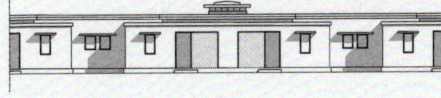

LIVING AREA: 60 MQ
PLINTH AREA: 78 MQ
VAIN: 7
PEOPLE: 6 /8

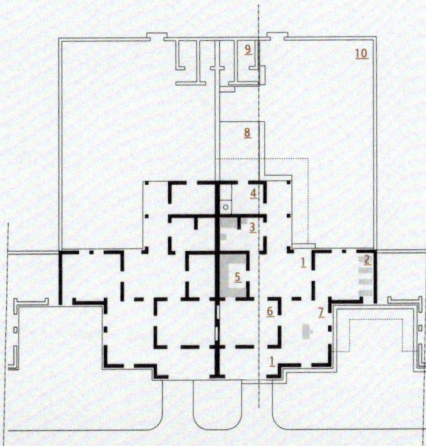

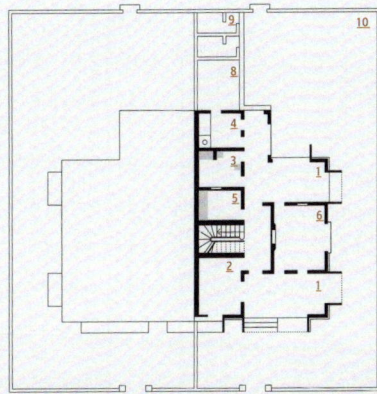

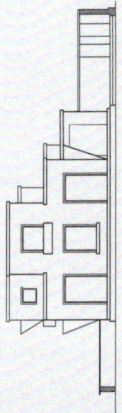

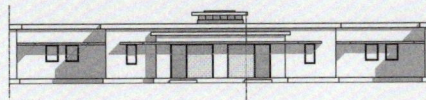

LIVING AREA: 71,4 MQ
PLINTH AREA: 89 MQ
VAIN: 8
PEOPLE: 10 /12

LIVING AREA:112 MQ
PLINTH AREA:158 MQ
VAIN: 7
PEOPLE: 6/8

1. VERANDA   3. KITCHEN   5. STORE   7. OFFICE   9. LAVATORY
2. BED ROOM   4. BATH   6. HALL   8. WASH PLATFORM   10. BACKYARD

0m   10m   20m

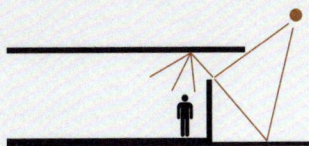

REFLECTED LIGHT, DIFFUSED
BY CEILING

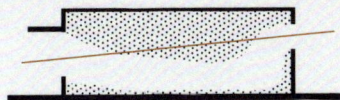

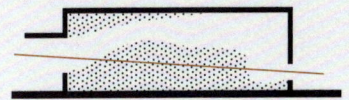

CANOPIES CAN ELIMINATE THE EFFECT OF PRESSURE BUILD-UP THE WINDOW, THUS THE PRESSURE BELOW THE
WINDOW WILL DIRECT THE AIR FLOW UPWARDS. A GAP LEFT BETWEEN THE BUILDING FACE AND THE CANOPY
WOULD ENSURE A DOWNWARD PRESSURE, THUS A FLOW DIRECTED INTO THE LIVING ZONE

Indian Architecture Building Democracy

4.
TIME
AND FEASIBILITY

/

THE MODERN SYSTEM was also the channel which gave each individual a possibility of social mobility and the means through which ideas and values such as equality and equal opportunity were diffused: a new transport system was introduced, offering access to the spaces of the city, now linked to an idea of modern social life which included the family, work and leisure. Theaters, libraries and recreational areas became the main places of socialization. The street was one of the most vital spaces in the city, and the setting for the main activities of daily life.

The real revolution consisted in the provision of systems for the supply of filtered water. Thus access to drinking water was guaranteed for the entire population, providing even the poorest inhabitants with one of the rights indispensable to survival. An incremental logic was applied to the roads and houses, which could be improved over time: provision was made for the enclosure of some parts of the house with light roofing and perforated walls.

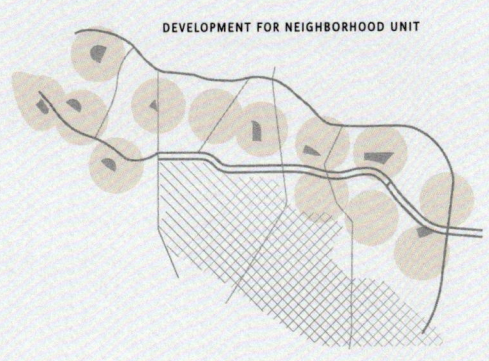

DEVELOPMENT FOR NEIGHBORHOOD UNIT

PUBLIC TRANSPORTS

HOUSIGN STREETS

WATERBODIES

BYPASS

INDUSTRY

CONTOUR LINES

ROADS

RAILWAY

800m

Indian Architecture Building Democracy

Balkrishna Vithaldas Doshi

MᴅᴬA — Thank you professor Doshi, to receive me in your beautiful Atelier and research institute. I am investigating the legacy of the Indian interpretation of Modernity in contemporary architecture.

Dᴏsʜɪ — My legacy I learned is that, be yourself. My guru only taught me that. Be yourself, think sensibly, and touch your heart before taking any decision. He never told me do this or do that. You are talking stylistically, it is not so. He influenced me by saying, "Be a free person".

DOSHI — We began in 1964, almost now 50 years ago, when India was developing because of industrialization, and new industries were being built. So it was usually built outside the town or the city. First you have to bring educated people to rural areas to manage the new technological things, you have to attract those people to areas where there are no cities and towns. So the issue is: they have to have, not sophisticated, but sufficient facilities. Not only a house but various types of houses because the income level, the skill level, and the job level are different. You have a manager, you have an executive, you have an officer, but you also have people working in the factory. All kinds of people were there and this was the first time an experiment was made of creating a township for 22.500 families. A large number are workers then there are officers, executives and managers. So you have social, cultural, economic differences among people, but there was one thing constant: the Indian way of life. The Indian way of life is different for people who work in the office and people who work at home, the ladies and the children and the social fabric in general.

In the kind of houses that we had to do, we had to find out how do you reduce apparent social disparity. It should not look like that house is for a big boss and there lives a worker. So the first question is: is it possible that from outside it should look similar but not necessarily the same? The next question was: there were not high technology things so you talk about cross-ventilation, cooling the house. Other problem: It was a standard plan but with variables so that they

A DIALOGUE WITH | BALKRISHNA VITHALDAS DOSHI

suited everybody differently, some people had gardens in their private house, some people were clustered with houses, with two storeys, single storey; and another consideration was plantation of lots of trees so you create shadow and shade and cooling areas. And yet you are away from the village and a town so you need also public activities: a school, a shopping bazaar, a garden and a good place they cannot get in a city, including hospital, maybe a little temple… This is really the kind of mechanics next which we had to work. You are working with a complex society and you have to put people of all hierarchies together.

So what is the key element in this? The key element are cultural activities and festivals, because in India, in festivals there are no barriers. So that network is in the open spaces. Open spaces, public spaces and the use of those public spaces. This is really how we began to think about housing, so one is economy of the house, (second) the sizes are varying but they have to be similar, third they have to be able to communicate with one another.

MD'A — What has brought (about) this? Your way of thinking about the project?

DOSHI — The whole idea is: when you have a settlement, the settlement must continue to add a new dimension of activity, and that activity must multiply. With the township like this, when we started in doing some other townships which we did in the 80s, Aranya Housing, they were the people that lived in the slums, they had come as migrants, they had nothing.
Those were four thousand families. So the government decided to give them houses but not a complete house, but only the plinth. Thirty square meters, and in that plinth you raise

this much bricks. Then they would have a water tap, electric connection a toilet built. After that they can have a kitchen made on their own. The toilet is available and the bathroom but the rest is only a plinth. So in that plinth they will build over time as they earn money. So the housing which was given was an attempt for subsidized houses, with little money to pay over twenty years, fifteen years.

They were migrants, there with no place. How do you really work out the economics?
But there are another four thousand families of slightly higher income group, who can be charged more money for the land. They can make some money there and pay back here. So there was this cross-subsidy.

Aranya was eight thousand families, but for the eight thousand families in Baroda and in Hyderabad we built the houses, but in Aranya we did not build the house. We said they will not have the money to pay, but as the money comes they will build, so over time they would buy a better canvas, they would buy bamboo, they would buy anything and make a shelter and when the money comes they will start building it with maybe bricks, etcetera.

This was the first time we started talking about a growing house, a house built by the owner, and they will build over five years, ten years, and slowly add because it has the services and yet the house. Everybody is now involved with the construction. Luckily they were not the same community, different religions, different community, different languages, and you can imagine eight thousand families, forty thousand people, and when eventually they doubled so eighty thousand people, two hundred acres of land, eighty hectares. This is how we built there, but there the advantage was that the house was built in such a way that they begun to expand. So we built there those houses and they became remarkable because they are the best houses I ever did because they were not designed by me. They grew and today you go there, you can't believe how beautiful and how wonderful life they have. People have skills, they have advantages of neighbors. After they built the house, they rented the lower place, they rented the upper place. The dimensions were designed by them so that they are minimum dimensions, there were no rules for that, so all houses are different and I thought that was the best thing that I have seen in the Indian tradition. So I came back to Indian tradition later, from '55 to '85.

Md'A — What we can learn about modernity?

Doshi — I think what I have learnt is that if you can provide good quality of life, and opportunity to improve the house, there are no barriers, and the architect is only incidental. So social anthropology, social attitudes are very important in designing houses and that is how we did the next housing. Then when we did large housing, like towns, next to Jaipur or next to Mumbay, Khargar, or maybe in Nagpur where there were three million people, two million people, half a million, fifty thousand, or Saibarabad , we found out this technique that you only do the main structure and allow the freedom to operate and most importantly remember that there should be no disparities but there must be opportunities for people, this is what it is.

Md'A — The incrementalism was born in India, what does that mean?

Doshi — It was there, it existed in India all along and I think I was probably one of the first to find this. Nobody has done incremental housing in the way I have done. It has not happened. I proposed this in the 50s-60s. It worked. Nobody has done this.

Mᴅ'A — During the years of the Independence Nehru chose for India to introduce Modernity. What did it mean?

Dᴏsʜɪ — It means that we have to understand the present, the scientific technological growth, which has affected our quality of understanding the world, our life and values. Modernity doesn't mean that you reject what is "the old" but you adopt the things which are better to improve the quality of life.

For me modernity is that you are updated with knowledge information, know what is happening today in the global world but yet you also have to have your roots to understand how much you absorb. According to me that is what Indian modernity is. ❡

A DIALOGUE WITH │ BALKARISHNA VITHALDAS DOSHI

A CAPITAL CITY
BHUBANESWAR

/

MADDALENA D'ALFONSO

Planned population: 50 000
1948 plan by Otto Koenigsberger

–

In Bhubaneswar a plan for the refoundation of the historic city was drawn up to turn it into the capital of the new state of Orissa (now known as Odisha). As at Chandigarh, the broader objective was to reorganize the territories of the federated states and the boundaries between them in one of the most depressed areas of India. The emergence of a movement for the formation of Orissa and the establishment of a new capital preceded independence and was the product of local forces that had organized themselves spontaneously.

The idea was that a new and modern city, built alongside a historical nucleus that had been in existence for 2500 years, would serve as a symbol of a federal, democratic and secular India that could stand next to the marvelous Kalinga monuments of the original center. In this way the elements of the local historical identity would have been able to merge with the more numerous and pluralistic ones included in the federal state.

The same stratagem was adopted in other urban schemes, and in particular the ones for federal capitals, where modern planning also had the objective of shaping a new Indian identity, in Chandigarh for instance.

The theme of modern planning as a means of proposing national cultural models is an important one in much Indian sociological literature.

In Bhubaneswar the band town model was put fully into effect, conforming to a clearly recognizable pattern at both the urban and the architectural level. The modernist inspiration of the plan is explicit in the vocabulary adopted in the technical report. Terms like traffic layout or shopping center were used, despite appearing out of context given the conditions existing at the moment of construction of the city. Thus Koenigsberger embarked on his work of training Indian professionals to respond to local problems by introducing Western instruments, planning practices and strategies, together with the diffusion of the new building technology that permitted the rapid and effective construction of new urban areas. He also consciously introduced Howard's model as mediated through American experience: the neighborhood unit was structured around a planned social and productive community, linked to an advanced system of public transport. In Koenigsberger's notes, moreover, there are references to American publications on the subject like "An Organic Theory of City Planning" by H. Herrey and C. Pertzoff, which appeared in Architectural Forum in April 1944.

The exceptional nature of this planning experience lies in the fact that the city was to be constructed entirely on government-owned land and with public money, so the intention was for the land and the housing units themselves to remain public property, and for their management and assignment to be handled by the organs of public administration.

The communities and people that were going to occupy the city were for the most part members of a lower middle class and middle class that would be employed in the administration of the federal capital and the surrounding region, distributed, in the plan of the city, according to a precise hierarchy that was reflected in the neighborhood units and in the layout of the grammar of modernity within them.

The hierarchy of the community can be discerned in the architectural composition of the housing and the schools, in the urban infrastructure, in the transport system and finally in the leisure facilities.

Each unit was of the same size and shape and had around 6000 inhabitants. Thus, just as at Jamshedpur, the band town assumed a regular configuration, predisposing the city in this way for a subsequent development that would be ordered in space as well as in time, in which the neighborhood unit represented the rule of composition.

Each unit was conceived both as a repeatable module in areas of future expansion and as a single nucleus based on the same principles of distribution, destined to have a development of its own. Each neighborhood would become an expression of the community that lived in it and that was responsible for its internal management. The residential buildings we find in the neighborhood units of Bhubaneswar adhere precisely to the architectural prototypes developed previously in Jamshedpur.

The formal solutions adopted by Otto Koenigsberger were the result of careful study of the climatic characteristics of the tropical country and of indigenous architectural techniques, with a recognition of the typical living conditions of the Indian people.

Building in the tropics means facing up to the inadequacy of Western techniques and standards, but above all dealing with the scarcity of resources, in both economic and material terms, and compensating for the backwardness of the means of construction. So the modernization of this reality had to start out from an awareness of these conditions.

Koenigsberger was a pioneer in India of the use of prefabrication, an extremely economic solution that facilitated the construction of buildings, responded to the urgent need to add to existing housing and stimulated the growth and productivity of the construction industry.

"Machine-built" houses were constructed using a slender framework of light steel, able to support part of the weight of the roof and permit its packaging, transport and assembly. The various parts were made out of local and easily obtainable materials and were designed in such a way that they could be bound together in simple packets of a rectangular shape that fitted without difficulty into railroad cars and trucks.

Providing these technical instructions, in line with Western city-planning practice and strategies, Koenigsberger continued his work of training Indian professionals and workers. We see here that he was laying the foundations of the incremental principle of aided self-help that would achieve a more complete definition in the planning of towns for refugees.

It is evident that all this reflected a desire for the democratization of urban space in a plan that made the most of the social and economic advantages of management of the city from the bottom up. Fully part of the debate over possible modernity in India, the project was carried out in an attempt to define an alternative way in which economic development could bring about a redistribution of wealth through spatial justice, based in this case on the public ownership of resources and the "right to the city".

urban mandala

BHUBA

ELISA FISCON

ESWAR

When Orissa was reunified in 1936 through the efforts of the Oriya regionalist movement, Bhubaneswar, a temple city and place of pilgrimage for Hindus, Buddhists and Jains, was chosen as its capital. It is located in the plains of northeastern India, between the fertile zone of the Mahanadi Delta and the jungle that covers much of the hinterland. The historical nucleus of shrines is concentrated around the sacred Bindusagar Tank and the temple of Lingaraja, dedicated to Shiva. In fact the city's name is derived from one of the god's epithets: Tribhuvaneshwara, or the Lord of the Three Worlds.

The modern city is located alongside the historic center, without any integration between them. Indeed, there is a clear separation between modernity and tradition. Its layout is linked to the preexisting infrastructure. The railroad marks the eastern limit and the airport its southern boundary, directing growth toward the north, where the ground is level and the regional road network provides a connection with Cuttack. The eight neighborhood units, each with an area of 180 hectares and intended to house 7000 people, are arranged in two parallel bands along the main traffic arteries. Each unit measures around 800 m on a side and was planned as a self-sufficient district, taking the needs of families into account. The population envisaged for the new capital was 50 000, a figure amply exceeded in the space of a few decades and which has now reached 837 000. The flexibility of the band town pattern made such rapid growth possible because of the way it permitted linear urban development.

1.
SECULARIZATION
AND ITS SOCIAL IMPACT
/

AN EMBLEMATIC CASE of outgrowing the religious city: the urban spaces of the Old Town are dictated by sacred rules of form and ritual, while the modern city alongside it answers, on the contrary, to requirements of rationality and functionality. Their relationship was conceived from the outset in a radical way: separated as an expression of different moments in history, but both recognizable and representative of the two souls of the city and the country.

The tension between cultural heritage and progress was reduced by the regionalist architecture of Julius Vaz. From the perspective of secularization, the new capital had to create collective spaces unaffected by religious distinctions, establishing points of reference that would be a reflection of the democracy which had been achieved. Thus civic centers, schools, libraries, theaters and public gardens assumed a central importance. These spaces were distributed in such a way as to act as links between the urban blocks.

	DWELLINGS		PARKS
	CIVIC CENTER		HOSPITAL
	CIVIC CENTER NOT REALIZED		AIRPORT
	RAPPRESENTATIVE CENTERS		EXISITNG CITY
	INDUSTRY		WATERBODIES
	PLAYGROUND		STREETS

800m

Indian Architecture Building Democracy

2.
DEMOCRACY AND THE REPRESENTATION
OF POWER

/

THE MASTER PLAN for the New Capital at Bhubaneswar was drawn up both for experts and for the inhabitants, who were called on to play an active part. The first part of the document consists of a written report and the second is composed of drawings. Together they show in a simple way the urban characteristics to be pursued.

The concept of popular government, necessary for the implementation of the plan, is explained in the introduction: active participation of citizens in the government of the city was required if the project was going to be a success, and so the document was circulated in order to encourage criticism from the bottom up and practical collaborations. The neighborhood units were designed with a spatial hierarchy that reflected the social one: there were different types of house and the largest were located close to the civic center or the major arterial routes. Each unit was to have a character of its own guaranteed by a system of self-government and self-improvement, and each community would have a representative in local government, allowing real democracy to be put in place.

10m 20m 30m

GREEN AREA

TREE

DWELLINGS

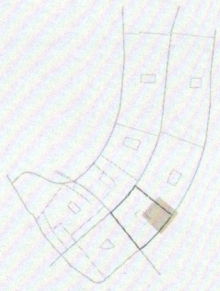

MASTERPLAN BY O. KOENIGSBERGER, 1948

Indian Architecture Building Democracy

3.
INDUSTRIALIZATION AND THE IMPACT OF TECHNOLOGY
/

THE LOGIC OF STANDARDIZATION was applied on an urban scale: the reproduction of the architecture of the housing, public buildings and schools assumed the characteristics of a genuine urban pattern. The houses followed closely the tropical prototypes of Jamshedpur. Each element was based on a spatial module designed to optimize the use of materials, the time of construction and the dimensions of the living quarters, along with systems of natural ventilation and protection from the tropical sun and the monsoon rains. Local materials like laterite, which offers significant advantages in construction, were used in the representative buildings.

However, the predominance of prefabrication and modern techniques, like reinforced concrete, relegated the red stone to a purely decorative role. Prefabrication relied on the emerging construction industry, a particularly transformative sector in 1950s Orissa.

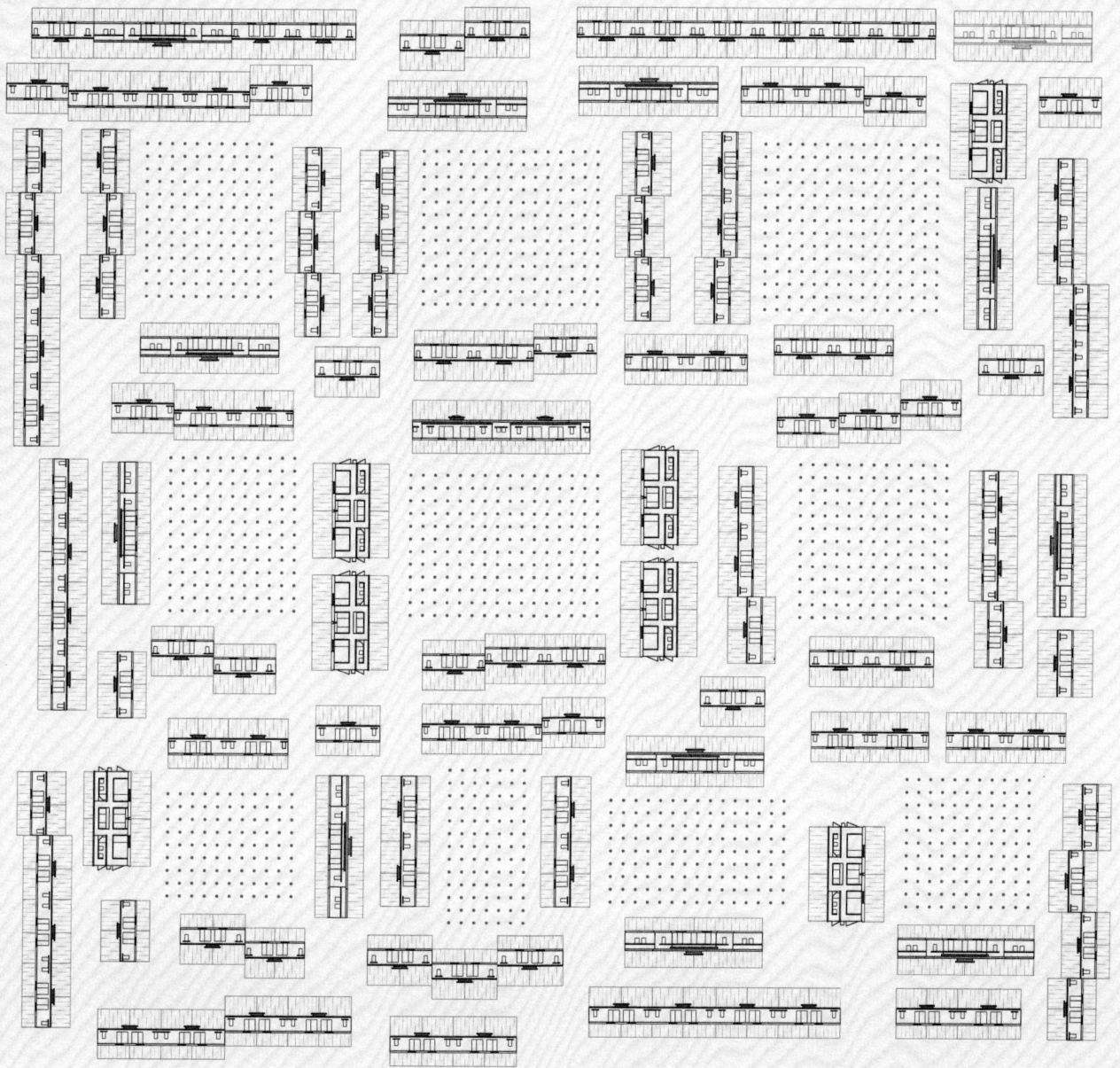

THE INTRODUCTION OF THE SECULAR PUBLIC SPACE WAS THE POINT OF ORIGIN OF THE NEW MODERN AND
DEMOCRATIC CITY. THE COMPLEX PROJECT OF SOIL PREDISPOSED THE COEXISTENCE OF WIDE OPEN SPACES, PUBLIC,
SEMI-PUBLIC AND PRIVATE. MADE ALSO POSSIBLE BY THE TYPE AND FORM OF HOUSING.

VEGETABLE GARDEN

TREE

HOUSES

4.
TIME
AND FEASIBILITY
/

THE PLANNING OF THE BAND town pattern was done in four dimensions, with the time factor taken into account along with the definition of space. The rhythm of daily life was marked out by locations—home, workplace and leisure facilities—as well as by movement between one place and another. The typology of housing was shaped by an incremental principle. It was possible to slowly adapt the spaces of the home to the growth and needs of the family.

In keeping with this logic of self-improvement the construction of the city was also planned in successive phases: in this way public funds were invested only where strictly necessary, in particular in the gradual expansion of major works of infrastructure, such as the linking of Bhubaneswar with Calcutta and Bombay and the building of the Hirakud Dam on the Mahanadi to meet the power needs of the city.

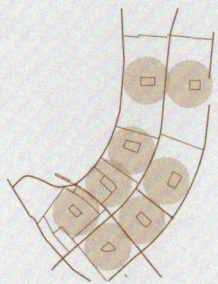

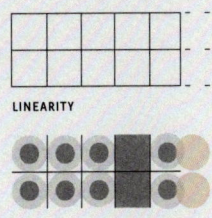

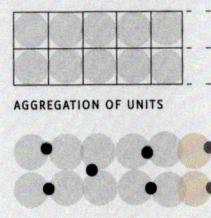

LINEARITY

AGGREGATION OF UNITS

- - - - - RAILWAY

━━━━━ REGIONAL ROADS

━━━━━ PRIMARY URBAN STREETS

──── SECONDARY URBAN STREETS

──── NEIGHBOURHOOD UNITS STREETS

■ WATERBODIES

800m

Indian Architecture Building Democracy

Krishna Menon

MDA — Thank you professor Menon to receive me. I am investigating the legacy of the Indian interpretation of the modernity in contemporary architecture.

MENON — A lot of us were educated abroad and so we came back with very firm ideas about modernity, and you try to implement and you try to learn something about what you've done. So what first I have to mention that our class almost had to de-school ourselves, de-school in a particular way, you confront reality, and then you de-school after confronting this reality.

For example I studied with Mies Van Der Rohe, I think I had a very good education but it is impossible to say that I work like Mies Van Der Rohe here. It's not possible. You try to absorb but you suddenly see it's quite different, a simple fact being that here things are put together first, in a much more unrefined manner not in the Miesian context of, you know, thinking things through and making sure it fits, making sure what will come out. Quite often what comes out is (something) that none thought of. So what I'm trying to tell you, this is school in itself, what are the new parameters that you'll follow, what are the new paradigms that you'll follow, what are the new objectives that you'll have. So these become issues that you need to be able to think about.…

Look at the recently curated exhibition on Raj Rewal. He is maybe the first or second generation of architects, at the National Gallery of Modern Art in Delhi. I tried to theorize the work of Raj Rewal… He is a very imaginative, very impressive architect. So this gap between what we set out to do and what we'll receive, is something that interests me because I think that this is something that education has to focus on, that practice has to focus on. So we started a new school of architecture to train each architect on confronting reality and being an architect.

MbA — Modernity associated with the personality of Nehru and with urban architecture in India has had a fundamental role in bringing the country to a position on the international scene. In this sense the case of Chandigarh is exemplary, although this is not considered as a city properly Indian.

MENON — Well, during the years soon after Independence, the role of Nehru in the introduction of modernity in India was fundamental. You should know that he was a very cosmopo-

litan person and he had a very cosmopolitan idea of modernity. He was a powerful leader, who could implement new ideas oriented to a future characterized by modern phenomenon in a country strongly linked to traditions.
In architecture, Nehru represents the will of innovation. He closed "the past" and opened "the future". He had a real obsession with technology. All his ideas were justified at that time, but today we know that they were wrong.
India has a very deep, varied and historical heritage in culture and architecture.

Therefore I believe it is wrong to speak today exclusively of modernity, to the future. I think that an architect must necessarily consider and relate himself with the past, but also with the future. Nehru's modernity demonstration is Chandigarh, a beautiful 'European city ' built in India, where the past is forgotten and the main objective is to give a possible vision of the future.

MD'A — BUT WHAT DOES IT MEAN?

MENON — The proposed solutions have solved some of the urban issues, but not the majority. Nehru introduced a powerful concept of modernity, capturing the imagination of people like us Indian architects, who have studied in occidental cultures and then come back to India.

Nevertheless his goals were very different in respect to the current ones, in particular in urban terms.
See, another thing is that India has been evolving and changing. It is evolving and changing very rapidly. What in Europe took a century or two centuries is happening in less than a decade, two decades. So it is difficult to assess what is ac-

tually happening, you think that something is happening but something else is happening. One of the terms that you used, one of the issues that you explained about an indigenous modernity, it's something that one is waking up to now, it has been happening thirty years but was not recognized that way.

MD'A — With modernity were imported design criteria, technical specifications for building and administrative procedures of financial management of the space for a partecipatory collectivity. Which aspects have been absorbed by Indian architecture and which ones have been rejected?

MENON — I think that the introduced direction is really positive, but I also recognize the fact that it has not happened. Our facilities, our technologies in construction, are identical to the ones used fifty years ago. Innovation happens only in determinate zones of the city, if one looks out, for example the preparation of the cement and its laying is still done by hand. Then in reality, when you say that in 1947 new technologies were imported and our culture has changed from thereon, it is not true. It has not happened.

The system remains as it was, it didn't change. Instead it is interesting to understand why it is unchanged, and the answer is because there are no resources and we are continuing with the most economic way, considering that it is better than the most technological way, because it costs less. Often the most economic way is also the worst one, for the reason that the system continues over the years and every time it is co-related with the discussion of economy. When one goes to, one sees super developments of an elite composed by really rich people and this doesn't change what we call the culture of the architecture, the culture of the construction. Talking about construction culture, the method introduced by the

A DIALOGUE WITH | A. G. KRISHNA MENON

modern movement remains, according to my personal point of view and with my analysis, just a media style which does not change this culture.

I believe that the modern movement has remained only a stylistic intervention, not cultural. For example, Le Corbuiser designed several houses for staff, but if you go to see how these people live in these neighborhoods, you recognize the difference between the conditions imagined instead by Le Corbusier for these people. He built a European kitchen, a European living room, a European bedroom. Modernity was created only on the stylistic level, was not created for the lifestyle.

MD'A — India has been an incredible laboratory to define the standards of tropical architecture. As a result, the solutions defined in the New Towns Protocol have migrated all over the world through foreign architects who took part in this movement. What is the credit that India today can redeem in other countries because of these models that have become a worldwide reference for tropical architecture and planning?

MENON — The idea that sees architecture as a tool for agencies (social engineering), I think is once again a truly modernist idea. The modern movement in Europe, through architecture, created a new society.

This same idea was brought here in India but it did not work because of strong differences between society and the various parameters of modernism. A real application of this kind of social engineering through architecture did not succeed. The direction taken continuously follows a culture of the past in a modern environment.

MD'A — In your opinion, what should be a way for a current Indian modernity?

MENON — It is a very big question! I think that one of the possible ways is to find the rules, this is the challenge, find the rules for becoming modern. I always speak of 'Indian exceptionalism', Something special has happened here, if we ignore completely all that we have, we become like any other country. Believe in what you have, I think this is the right direction. For example in urban planning, development and urbanization are equal. If you develop, you urbanize and in all parts of the world this takes place. But in India we urbanize without developing.

Why? Consider the case of Jamshedpur, we urbanized them but we did not develop. The link between the people who live in cities and villages is very strong, and in China also the link is very strong, but the difference between China and India is that we are a poor country, we have a strong democracy and we are evolving, changing, nothing is static and nobody understands how we are evolving, how we are changing. So what happens to a city is very difficult to predict.

The coordination between urbanization and development is something that should be studied and understood. Before doing this, we cannot answer the question, "What should India do?". ¶

A DIALOGUE WITH | A. G. KRISHNA-MENON

A TOWN FOR REFUGEES
FARIDABAD

/

MADDALENA D'ALFONSO

Planned population: 50 000
1949 plan by P.L. Varma

–

IFaridabad is an emblematic case of a new Indian town. In fact it is a particularly interesting case from the perspective of folk planning. Emerging out of a transit camp for refugees set up on the outskirts of New Delhi, its conception and construction were based on the principle of "aided self-help," a theme already tackled in the project for Bhubaneswar and one that was developed fully here. It was configured as a satellite town of the capital, intended to lighten the demographic burden of the refugees from Pakistan and to reduce the pressure from the migration into the city of a large number of people from the surrounding countryside. In fact the Punjab, located close to the capital Delhi, was one of the regions most affected by the drama of Partition.

Nehru's new government had finally approved the new towns protocol and given Otto Koenigsberger the post of advisor, from where he could promote the National Congress's ideal of a new democratic India, made up of free citizens thanks to the construction of cities. In this case O. Koenigsberger, in the role of supervisor, provided support and training for the team responsible for the town while the actual planner was P.L. Varma, a Punjabi engineer and the man who would be charged with recruiting a Western architect for the project of Chandigarh. So Faridabad was of one of the first towns planned by an Indian.

The design put into effect was a particular version of the band town pattern. From the architectural perspective, Faridabad opened reflection on a twofold question: on the one hand, the context was taken into account and a planning of the landscape promoted, with a sinuous design that attempted to give a settled form to the city, making the most of the topographic and botanical qualities of the territory as a whole; on the other, questions were asked about the relationship between the social dimension and the city, and for this reason preference was given to a closed form, understood as a common nucleus around which to organize the numerous community groups and the complex family units, treated as social cells in keeping with Geddes's vision. This result was achieved by expanding the space separating the two bands to create an empty space at the heart that could be used for the institutions on an urban scale around which the neighborhoods were laid out. A railroad line linking the new center with the capital ran along the east side of the town. The linear pattern of the band town model was maintained in the subsequent development of the town, thanks to the very strong relationship with the road and rail infrastructure that, as time has passed, has made it a direct extension of Greater Delhi.

Being a town for refugees, with a planned population twice that of Bhubaneswar, the neighborhood unit was no longer a quadrangular element that was repeated in a linear fashion, but was divided up internally into smaller nuclei. The large dimensions of the units would facilitate an expansion of Delhi while guaranteeing at the same time the connection to the center of the capital with surface lines of public transport.

Although it was O. Koenigsberger's intention, inspired by the utopian ideas of Gandhi, for the town to make the processing of agricultural produce the hub of its economy, he was already conscious in 1948 that its geographical location and the infrastructure that was being put in place would make Faridabad an ideal location for industrial activities, and this is what in fact happened.

The most innovative aspect of this experience, however, was the construction of an ideal town that was rooted in the concept of incremental growth and "aided self-help." Thanks to the collaboration between O. Koenigsberger and P.J. Varma particular attention was paid here to the question of the development of Indian expertise that could be brought to bear over time on the problems of planning, management and maintenance of the territory. So what characterized this experience was the process of the town's construction, in which planners, other professionals and refugees were all involved. 20 000 volunteers were chosen from a group of refugees to start the building of a new community in a new social and urban context. In this way associations of farmworkers, operators of kilns for the production of bricks, workers specialized in the construction of roads, bricklayers and carpenters were set up. Most of these cooperative artisans during the construction of the town and its development and the associations would last in time grown.

So the fundamental point was that, alongside the construction of the town, a productive community developed, with the integration of its members, through vocational training, into a new social as well as urban context. In Otto Koenigsberger's version of folk planning, the narrative and romantic aspect that characterized Geddes's idea was set aside, in order to turn the people involved into architects of the change in their own social and professional lives. In the neighborhood unit Otto Koenigsberger saw not only practical advantages for growth and the simple regulation of traffic but also educational effects on society, which would be able to attain a new civic level by living in salubrious communities: "The main objectives of neighborhood unit planning are however not so much practical advantages [...] but the pedagogical effects which are expected from the system. Neighborhood units are intended to improve and strengthen the feeling of civic responsibility among the inhabitants." One of the advantages of the self-construction of the town was the introduction among the inhabitants of means that could be used for democratic participation in the administration of the city: for this purpose it was proposed that civic representatives be elected to take responsibility for order and cleanliness in their neighborhood. Koenigsberger's idea was to create a community based on collaboration among the inhabitants and their involvement in the shaping of a new society, commencing with the planning, management and maintenance of their own neighborhood unit. This aspect of the operation is crucial to understanding the shift in the focus of interest of modern architecture from the end product to the processual aspect, thereby anticipating one of the great questions of contemporary life.

players and playgrounds

MADDALENA D'ALFONSO

ABAD

During Partition 4.7 million refugees moved from the new state of Pakistan into Northwestern India. Delhi attracted the largest numbers, and to limit the demographic pressure on the capital the government launched the Pakistani Refugee Resettlement Project, setting up refugee camps in areas where it would be possible to exploit existing infrastructure–the Delhi-Mathura-Agra national highway and the Delhi-Bombay railroad line–to construct towns like Panipat, Yamuna Nagar, Gurgaon, Jhajjar, Sonipat, Rohtak and Faridabad. The latter is a unique case in the process of indigenization of modernity by means of the band town pattern: it represented the first implementation of a participatory paradigm.

The starting point was a camp of around 20 000 people who, through folk planning, made an active contribution to the construction and administration of the new town. The layout of the town around the temporary settlement made possible the reallocation of the refugees in phases. The town was made up of five neighborhood units, each housing about 4000 people in around 60 hectares.

The planned settlement was laid out on state-owned land, while the actual housing units were to be built by the inhabitants. This was supposed to give people an incentive to settle permanently, taking up the opportunity to live in a small modern town with services like schools and hospitals. Faridabad was to be a reflection of the desires and wishes of its residents, the real engine of the process of construction of the new democratic society.

1.
SECULARIZATION
AND ITS SOCIAL IMPACT
/

PUBLIC SPACE was introduced starting from the open heart around which the built-up area was organized. This was slowly emptied of the temporary accommodation of the refugees as the town was constructed, becoming a large area of parkland in which the main public institutions were located: a manifesto of the new, modern city. An awareness of the pluralism of the different cultures present in India determined the need for a new space, accessible to the population without any limitations apart from those of civil coexistence. In these open and green playgrounds were to be located all the primary services required by a self-sufficient community.

The houses, moreover, were built on public land divided up into lots that were the same size for everyone. The basic premise, therefore, was the principle of social equality and the idea that all the individuals in society should have the same rights: access to education, health care and other fundamental social rights like security, the vote, freedom of speech and association and the right of ownership. Only in this way would it be possible to create a society able to develop a social identity of its own, along with a sense of belonging to the place that would make Faridabad a town to all intents and purposes.

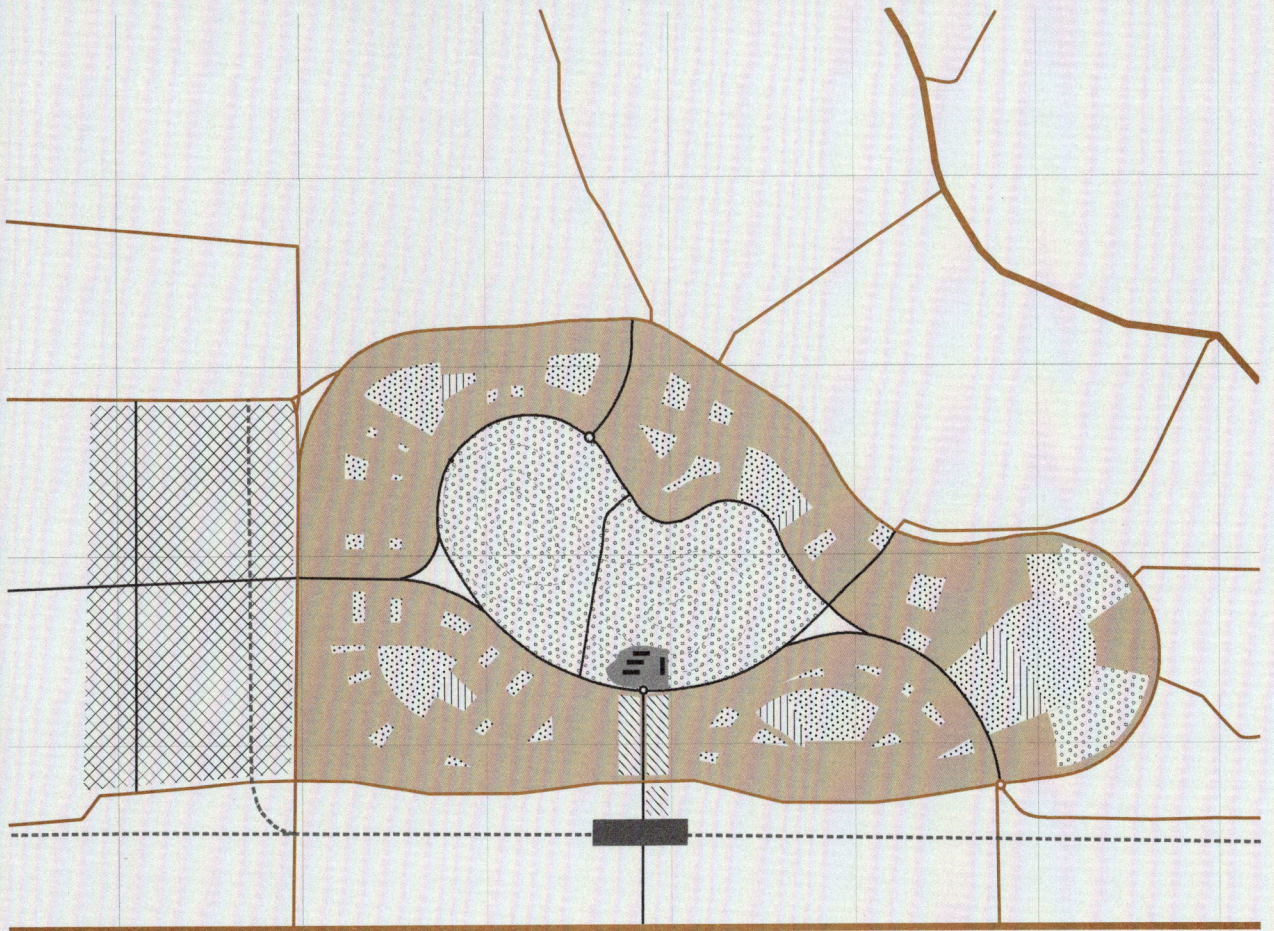

DWELLINGS

CIVIC CENTER

RAPPRESENTATIVE
CENTERS

INDUSTRY

PLAYGROUND

GREE CORE

STREETS

RAILWAY

800m

2.
DEMOCRACY AND THE REPRESENTATION
OF POWER
/

ON THE ONE HAND folk planning stemmed from study of the traditional Indian way of life, the characteristics of the tropical climate and all the problems linked to the construction of new towns in profoundly underdeveloped contexts; and on the other from a desire, on the part of the planner, to consider the inhabitants the real players to mobilize in the field, along with their interests and wishes.

The democratization of space was in the first place represented by the circularity of the city's development: its closed and no longer linear design meant that its growth was limited and circumscribed. The infrastructures were designed, in fact, so that each point of the town would be equidistant from the center. In addition, the railroad station—in the original plan—was supposed to be as central as possible, while the railroad line ran at a tangent to the town in the east. Finally, a line of public transport by road ran around the large empty space at the center, with the aim of connecting the various parts of the city in an easy and rapid manner.

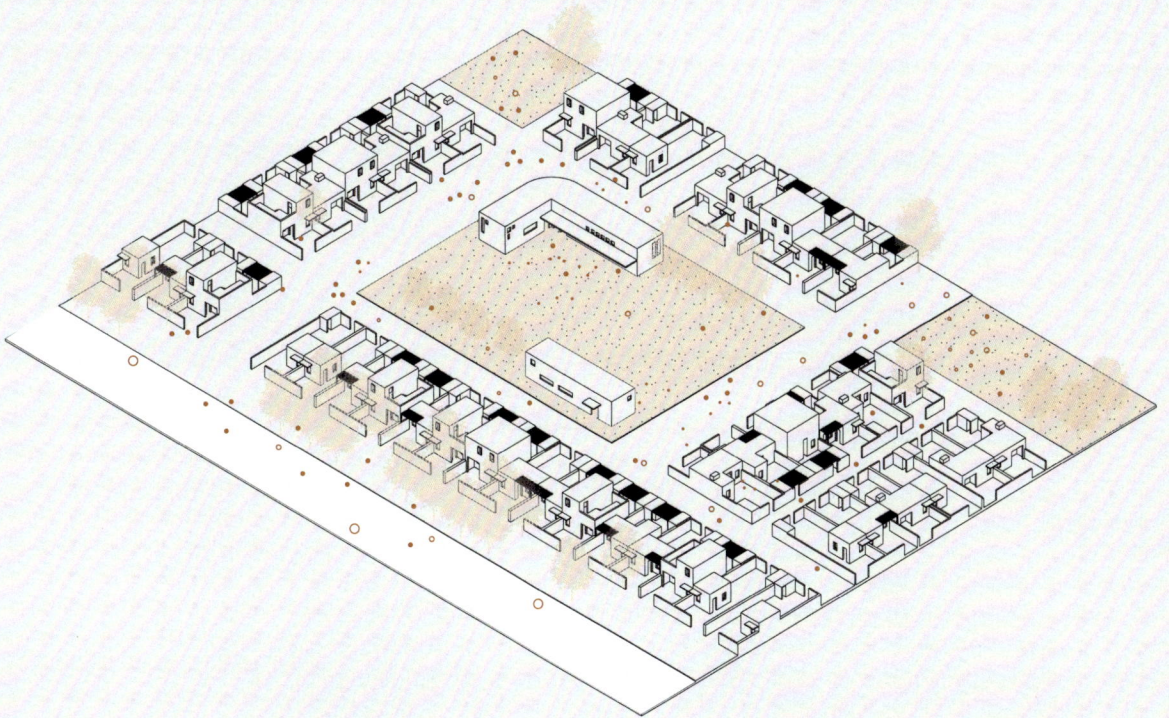

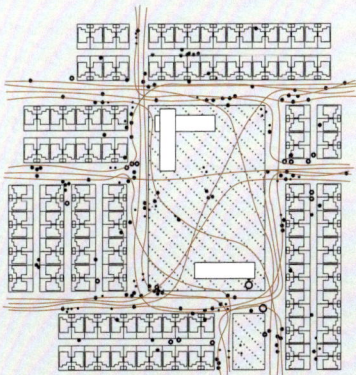

THE BAND TOWN PATTERN ARTICULATES BUILT AROUND
LARGE PUBLIC OPEN SPACES.
THE DRAWING OF TRAFFIC PREDISPOSES THE COEXISTENCE
OF PEOPLE, CHILDREN AND ANIMALS
THROUGH THE DIFFERENTIATION OF ROADS AND PATHS.

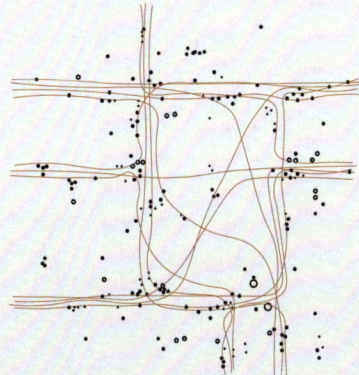

EACH NEIGHBORHOOD PROMOTES INTEGRATION
AND THE MEETING FOR EVERY AGE
DUE TO THE PRESENCE OF SCHOOLS, SURGERIES
AND SPACES FOR LEISURE.

☐ HOUSING UNITS		•	PEOPLE
▨ CIVIC CENTER: SCHOOL, OFFICES, ETC...		·	CHILDREN
— FLUXES		∘	SMALL ANIMALS
		○	LARGE ANIMALS
		◯	EXTRA LARGE ANIMALS (EX. ELEPHANTS)

3.
INDUSTRIALIZATION AND THE IMPACT
OF TECHNOLOGY
/

THE CONSTRUCTION of the town was used as an opportunity to reeducate the refugees for new productive occupations: programs of self-help for the population were devised, aimed at giving them the means to learn an activity and make a living from it. So the role of the planner was to provide a practical guide to constructing the home out of elements as if it were a 'kit'. Artisans and professionals were organized into associations and cooperatives.

Thus workers were trained in brickmaking, woodworking and other skills useful for the construction of roads and houses, something that would permit the growth of the city in stages, through mass production of the elements. On the basis of industrial entrepreneurial schemes, the Indian state gave concessions and provided funds for the setting up of factories and manufacturing activities that would create jobs for the refugees in the future, when the ones connected with the construction of the town began to diminish.

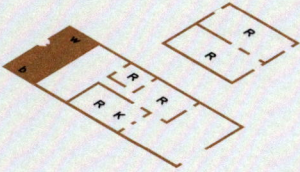

5 STEP
2 FLOOR HOUSE
4 ROOMS
LIVINGROOM
KITCHEN
TOILET
BATHROOM

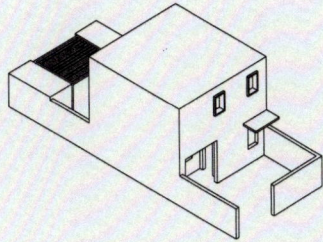

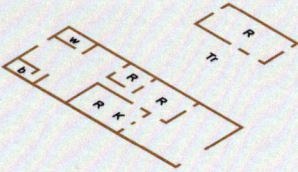

4 STEP
2 FLOOR HOUSE
3 ROOMS
LIVINGROOM
KITCHEN
TOILET
BATHROOM

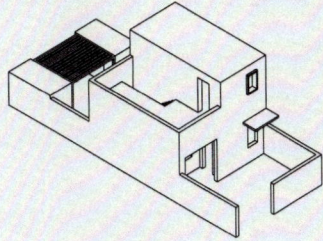

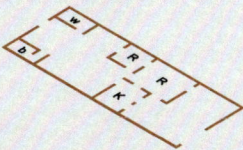

3 STEP
2 ROOMS
LIVINGROOM
KITCHEN
TOILET
BATHROOM

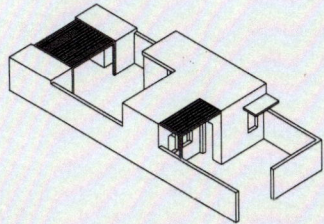

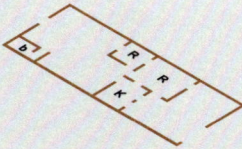

2 STEP
2 ROOMS
KITCHEN
TOILET

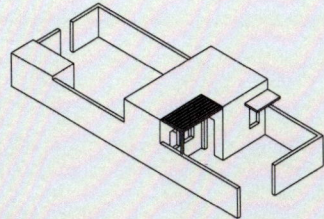

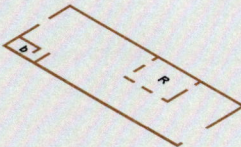

1 STEP
1 ROOMS
TOILET

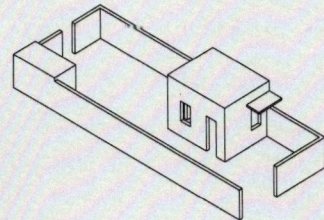

R: ROOM / K: KITCHEN / B: TOILET / TR: TERRACE

Indian Architecture Building Democracy

4.
TIME
AND INCREMENTALISM
/

P.J. VARMA PAID particular attention to the processual and operational aspect of the construction of the new town and showed an appreciation for practices of self-improvement. This was a process that triggered a change in the attitude of the society and of people to time. The majority of the population involved in the construction of Faridabad was provided with training and an opportunity to update its skills. The new government guaranteed the workers additional subsidies that boosted their pay to as much as 150% more than the normal cost of labor on the market.

This mode of conceiving the town made possible, in fact, the creation of a participatory society, in which the incremental aspect took on particular importance, from the level of housing to the urban scale. The home, turned into a place for delocalized work, served as a workshop of mass production as well as a dwelling. Houses were provided with a story that could be used as a small workspace or store where the residents could carry out their activities. Architectural incrementalism was in fact linked to the economic growth and family plans of each individual.

ABSTRACT LAYOUT OF A NEIGHBOURHOOD UNIT

	CIVIC CENTER		HOUSING UNIT 30MQ 2/4P
	UPPER FLOORS RESIDENCES		HOUSING UNIT 70MQ 6/8P
	INCREMENTAL DEVELOPMENT UPPER FLOORS		HOUSING UNIT 90MQ 10/12P
	TREES		HOUSING UNIT 120MQ 6/8P
	HOUSING STREET		CONSERVANCY LANES

EXPORTING
MODERNITY

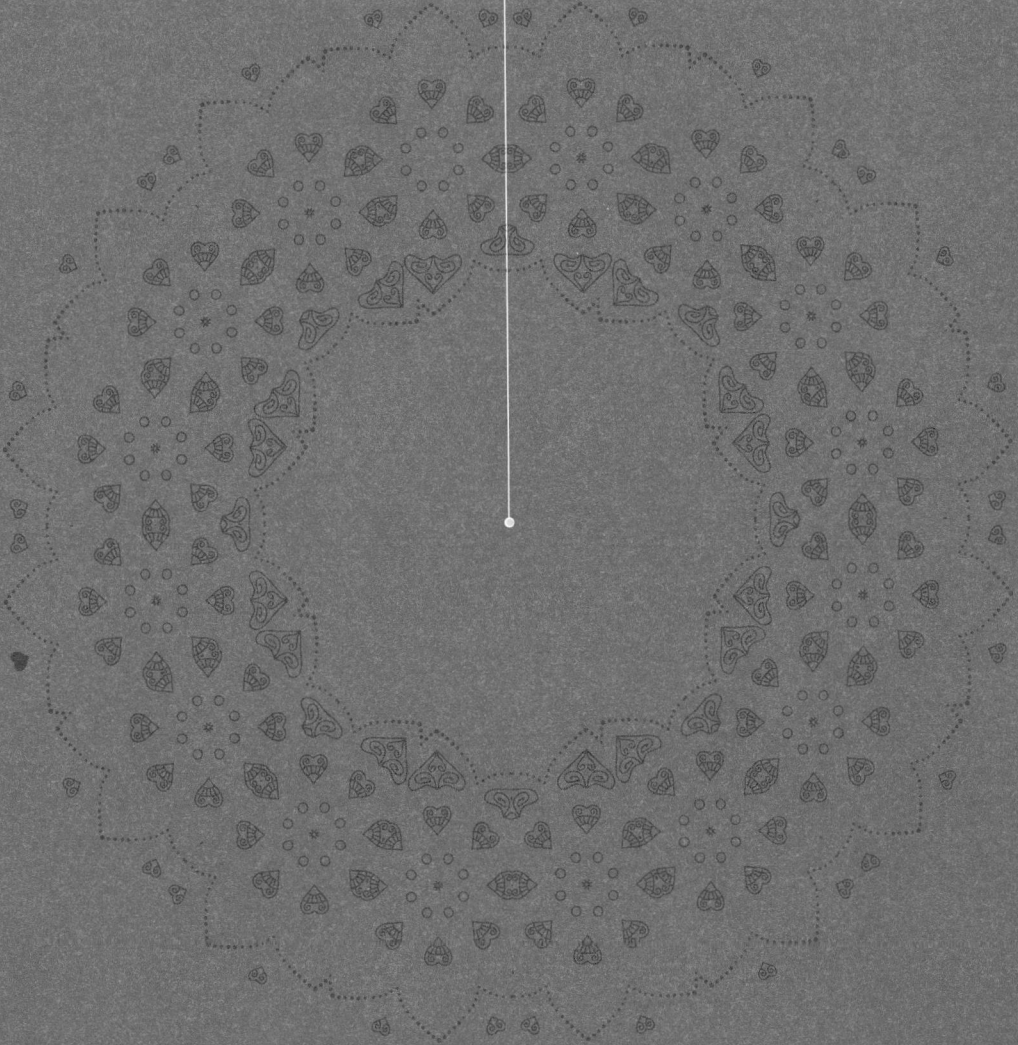

Indian Architecture Building Democracy

Redrawing chandigarh

/

PHOTOGRAPHY BY MARCO INTROINI

The realization that Chandigarh was the peak of a new sensibility in architecture and city planning that has seen modernity adapt itself to completely different climatic contexts and cultural identities from the ones that existed in Europe and the West makes it possible to regard it as the first step toward an appreciation of the vast extent of the territories in which tropical modernity would be able to produce radical changes.

Chandigarh can be seen as the first widely recognized case of the export of the modern tropical paradigm, replete with architectural and aesthetic models that were shared with the elite of the time.

Indian Architecture Building Democracy

GUEST
4/6 DELUXE ROOM

BUSINESS

ROOM No.45 ROOM No.46

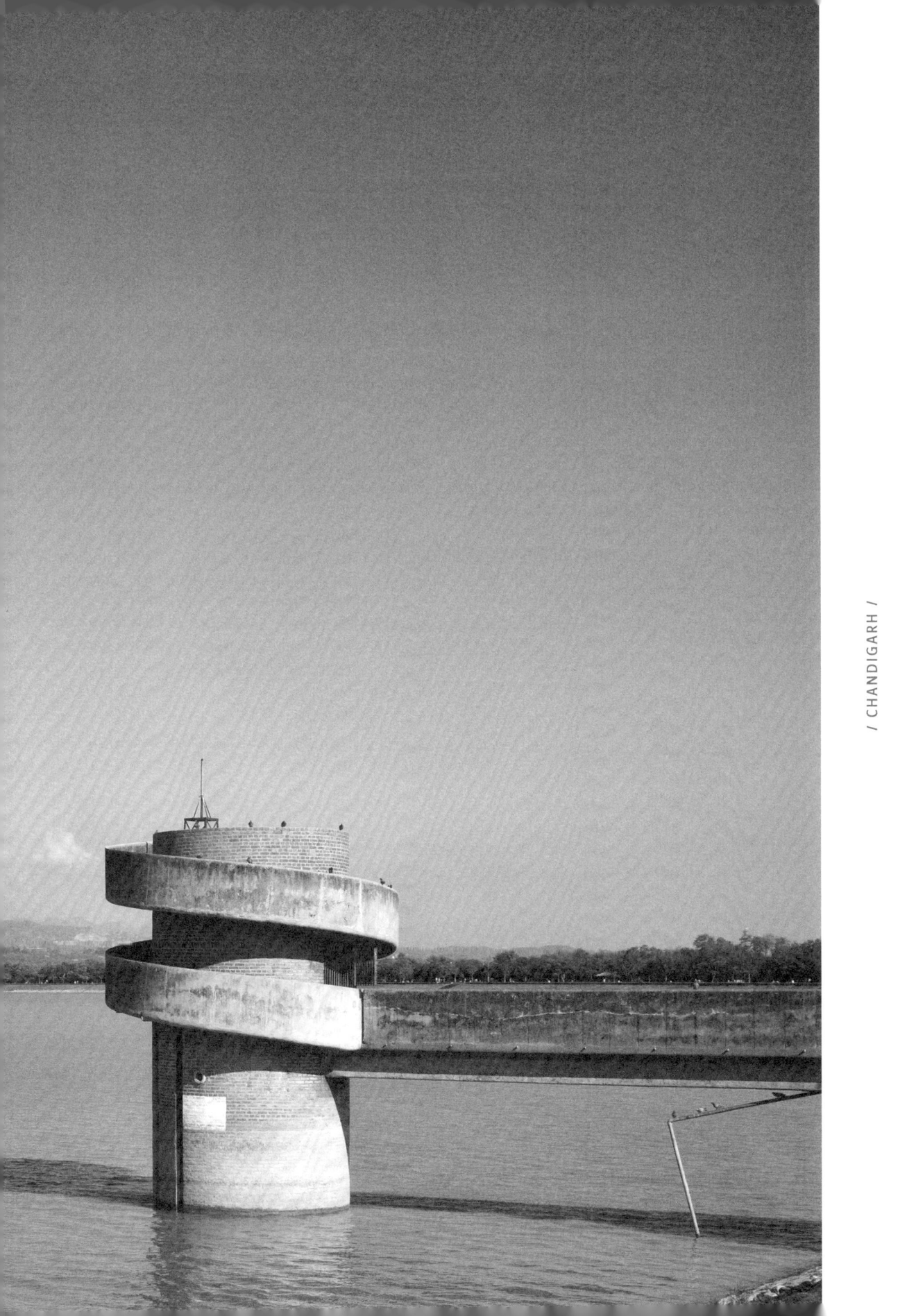

WHAT ARE WE TALKING ABOUT WHEN WE SPEAK OF PARTICIPATORY ARCHITECTURE? THE INDIAN ROOTS

/

MADDALENA D'ALFONSO

A Year of Revolutions
–

The year 1960 has come to be known as the Year of Africa: seventeen nations were formed as a consequence of a rapid process of independence that made decolonization a concrete and tangible fact, culminating in the declaration condemning colonialism that was approved by the United Nations on December 14 of the same year.

And so the question of the future of an unfathomable and mysterious land was finally raised: a continent whose ambiguous oscillation between credible opportunity for modernization and actual archaism was alarming.

What now stirred people's consciences, drowsing under the tepid sun of the alternation of four seasons typical of temperate climes, had for hundreds of years awakened the instinct of adventurers. Not all of them, however, had been driven by an unscrupulous colonial attitude. There were also those who, motivated by socialist ideals or a libertarian and egalitarian spirit, had embarked on an adventure for different reasons. This is demonstrated by that paradigm of architecture and modern city planning which establishes a close relationship between aesthetic standards and the project of modernization in contexts of social backwardness.

These men and women have had a decisive influence on the course of the history of the city and architecture. They initiated changes in people's daily lives through the use of space, technology and all the means available for the construction of a new order, attuned to human beings. Retracing the paths they followed makes it possible to open a new debate on the legacy of modern participatory architecture. As has already been said, there was in fact a noble prelude to the concept of modern architecture, synonymous with rights-based architecture, that was applied in postwar architectural and urban history by marginal and non-European (*decolonized*) countries.

From Western Centers to Tropical Peripheries
–

If on the one hand the paradigm of center and periphery can help us to understand the political relations between territories, on the other it makes evident their complexity and the mutual dependence of one on the other. It can be said in fact that, historically, the relationship has been characterized by a transfer of innovation on the basis of shared cultural principles from the center to the periphery. When the emphasis is placed instead on economic aspects, it becomes clear, notwithstanding the interdependence between the poles of the system, the extent to which the peripheries depend on centers without any possibility of them breaking away and surviving on their own.

There is a third way that places the emphasis on the organizational aspects of the bureaucratic regulations and protocols that usually promulgate from the center to the fringes of the territory, resulting in practice in a uniform adjustment that can be defined as top-down. However, this third point of view also permits its inversion and analysis of the Indian case makes this evident. It is perhaps the first example of a bottom-up process on a global scale: the protocols developed for social and technological adaptation and formalized and standardized in the marginal setting of the Indian territory have been studied and promoted in Western centers—e.g. the United Nations and the AA, UCL and LSE in London—or directly applied in other territories on the fringes.

The debate over how to intervene in non-European contexts and in Africa in particular was already lively between the wars, when conferences were organized by the International Federation for Housing and Town Planning (IFHTP), a nongovernmental organization founded by Ebenezer Howard in 1913 with the aim of exchanging knowhow and techniques on questions regarding new settlements and city planning. The countries involved were Britain, France and Germany, three of the major colonial powers.

The starting point for the IFHTP's reflection was the idea of promoting better living conditions for people and setting in motion processes of participation in public life, thereby linking the question of the management of what Carlo De Carli called primary space to the political dimension and the sense of belonging. This vision generated an idea of reciprocity between place, services, structures and the acceptance by the population of a system of order and government. The principal objectives of the overall design of urban settlements were inevitably those of hygiene and control. The organic visions were the utopia of the ideal city on a human scale, Howard's garden city, and the model of the Siedlungen that would be tried out later by Ernst May in Frankfurt.

The most interesting conference was the one held in Berlin in 1925, whose subject, "Slums," is indicative of the faith in the possibility of bringing about change and improvement on the basis of a reflection on inhabited spaces. The examples presented regarded for the most part interventions in the European city, but the themes discussed came out of a more general vision that still saw colonial cities as an opportunity for trying out the new ideas. Emblema-

tic of this aspect was the presentation of a project in Palestine, which had been a burning issue for Britain since 1920. The new chapter opened by this global view of the problems of the city and of human settlements was brought to an abrupt halt by the outbreak of war in 1939. By the time peace returned in 1945 the geography and balance of power were completely different and the slow process of decolonization was soon to get under way, promoted by now rigidly defined ideologies, able to operate with new instruments and technologies that opened up possibilities of massive change.

The growth of the building industry, urban development and the founding of new towns, along with the construction of new infrastructure for transport, resulted in the propagation of a global version of modernity in response to similar problems in all parts of the world, independently of the actual context in which they were situated.

At the end of the Second World War, in fact, the world was reconstructed to fit the balance of power symbolized by the Iron Curtain, a conflict whose theater now lay outside the continent of Europe. The configurations that rapidly emerged depended on fragile alliances typical of wartime needs, but generated the slow and unrelenting process of decolonization, in a climate still unprepared for the entry of new sovereign nations, like the ones in the Indian subcontinent and the Middle East, and still strongly tied to colonial habits and a management of resources and advantages based on extraterritorial logic. The difficulties in the monolithic management of Africa and the Middle East were made evident by a symbolic act: the founding of the state of Israel in 1948. Which led to a clear distinction in the international strategies adopted to deal with the Middle Eastern question and postcolonial transition in Africa. In the period leading up to the decline of the "colonial empires," there are two strictly disciplinary aspects that need to be pointed out: on the one hand architecture became the primary instrument of urban planning, not just in the context of the welfare states in postwar Europe, but also in countries still under the colonial yoke and above all those in the process of decolonization, in transition toward independence; on the other there was the conviction that it was possible to control by phases and programs the progress toward the founding of new and democratic societies through top-down strategies.

In fact the combination of the need for control, processual practices and aesthetic norms resulted basically in a negotiation of modernity to fit the context. While in Africa the persistence of the colonial system favored the logic of a modernization aimed at the stripping of resources and the housing of substantial numbers of migrants in the cities of the various empires, in the Indian subcontinent and in India in particular, as we have seen, a methodology of intervention was developed to implement the precise desire for a democratization of architecture starting out from the architecture itself.

A methodology that would later be adopted by the United Nations [4] to tap into and facilitate processes of postcolonial democratic transition.

Mobilization of the Peripheries
–

Cities have always been constructed through the grafting on of ideas and projects that have migrated until they found a place where they could be tried out and put into effect. An open-minded place willing to experiment with the potentialities offered by the new configuration of the relations among parts, structured through space, in the scaling of places, in the arrangement of accesses, in the spread of service networks, in the distribution of wealth, in the density of housing and in the accessibility of open space and the surrounding territory. At other times ideas have circulated until they came across extreme situations, ready to risk everything in order to introduce change through the power of space and unconditional trust in the management of it.

So it is possible to regard the Indian case as exemplary of a current of thought about architecture and the city that set out to realize a vision through ideal models, taken up by independent governments. The planning solutions, which in that case were the outcome of a liberation achieved through peaceful revolution, were then transferred to the rest of Asia, to Africa and to South America through the planners and architects who adhered to the United Nations' programs of development in tropical environments. This happened because the first Indian government asked Otto Koenigsberger, [5] the German architect who was active in India in the years around Independence, to find sustainable solutions for the modernization of the country. Working under the Ministry of Health he summoned experts from all over the world and developed an urban model versatile enough to adapt to Indian customs. This paradigm, known as the "band town pattern," seemed equally suited to application in Africa and in all the other pre-modern regions that were awaiting a solution to similar problems. For that matter, without industrialization and globalization, the revolution in customs could not have borne fruit.

In the ferment that saw, therefore, architecture at the forefront in the definition of feasible new social models, the city and the relationship between city and territory began to play a decisive role. Through cities it was possible to take control of large populations and numerous ethnic groups, to manage resources and the optimization of production and finally to bring about a change in lifestyles and socioeconomic relationships.

The city as such became the battleground and true protagonist of the negotiation of modernity in the second half of the 20th century, and modern architecture served as its preeminent tool of implementation, owing to its original nature, eternally poised between means of control/segregation and utopian ideal. Signs of this can be found all over the world and it is legitimate today to study the results in order to see which spaces proved capable of implementing people's rights, what ideas can be picked up and used to reexamine and make the most of democratic participatory space, which approaches can be considered relevant in the present and what perspective on participatory democracy has been handed down to us by modernity.

The Centrality of Marginality
–

I believe that a possible answer can be found in the legacy of the architects who have worked on the growth of cities in non-Western countries, characterized by their location in the tropical climatic belt, whose similar concerns led to the emergence of an autonomous reflection on architecture that reached its peak in the Tropicalismo [6] of Niemeyer and Lúcio Costa's Brasilia. [7]

To conceive a sustainable future, therefore, it is necessary to reconsider history. And we will look at that history of architecture for the city and the development of an expertise for the Non-Aligned Countries, as Nehru and Tito • [8] called them when, after the Second World War, they looked for a way of avoiding the onerous alliance offered by the two power blocs and finding an alternative route to development for a diverse range of new nations. At the same time these nations were dubbed Third World Countries • [9] by the economist Alfred Sauvy, a label which he applied to all the developing countries, and not just the newly independent former colonies, located chiefly in the southern hemisphere, that were trying to find an autonomous and practicable socioeconomic model.

Out of the search for an alternative approach to planning arose the first debate between the supporters of the idea of an industrialized urban environment as the most effective model and those who saw a rural-urban mix as a possibility for sustainable and widespread development: a lively sociopolitical dispute fought out by the followers of Nehru and Gandhi respectively. In India there was on the one hand a substantial migration to urban centers, resulting in large spontaneous settlements, and on the other a large proportion of the population that remained in rural villages, making it necessary to improve conditions in the latter.

Gandhi's position • [10] was to propose the strengthening of agriculture and handicrafts in the villages untouched by modernization, while Nehru • [11] regarded the city as a means for the redistribution of wealth and development of the poorest areas of the nation. This debate, as we have seen, led to the definition of a protocol in India for the founding of hundreds of small and middle-sized towns, which would be able to redistribute assets, provide education and health services and impart new skills to a population which at that time was unprepared to handle the complexity of a democracy and the educated participation that this required. In short, the choice was made to show faith in progress as a means of emancipating the social classes. We can look at India as an incredible experimental laboratory, where Western knowhow was called on to train an elite of Indian professionals, capable of absorbing the teachings and then using them to shape and consolidate an original and autonomous approach.

The Tropical Periphery and the Adventurers
–

The history of architecture and the history of the city as well as that of territories has been written through the linking of symbolic episodes, often in reference to monumental architecture. Although the history of ideas needs succinct moments that bring scientific discoveries and the related aesthetic results together in a "here and now," its course is much more uneven and varied. These discoveries are often the fruit of experiments that result from a sophisticated dialogue between core and peripheries, made possible by people who are willing to move between places. People who often appreciate the fact that in locations on the fringes, where there may be no direct control, it is possible to find unique opportunities to make a concrete contribution to global change.

Otto Koenigsberger, Jane Drew, Maxwell Fry, • [12] Le Corbusier, Pierre Jeanneret, Albert Mayer and later Louis Kahn were all involved in study of the local situation with the aim of defining a paradigm of urban development and an architectural language for the future of India. Each of them arrived with an international theoretical perspective and a mature Western aesthetic and through Chandigarh •, [13] the last and biggest city covered by the protocol, came up with a renewal of the aesthetic characteristics and prospects of the processes of construction of modernity. Otto Koenigsberger, an exile from Nazi Germany who had sought refuge in India, where he was granted citizenship *(a status he would retain until the 1990s)*, was in charge of drawing up the protocol on behalf of the Ministry of Health

Jane Drew and Maxwell Fry, already active in the IFHTP, had had an opportunity to study and try to understand systems of social life based on ancient customs in the African villages of the Gulf of Guinea and claimed to have specific expertise that allowed them to operate in depressed situations verging on endemic poverty.

Le Corbusier had already made a second visit to Algiers and drawn up his plan for the city

(Plan Obus, 1930-31), as well as two trips to Brazil in 1929 and 1936, when he had made contact with Lúcio Costa and Niemeyer over the project for the Ministry of Health and Education.

Albert Mayer, an American architect and planner, had developed a housing policy for the US government (1937) and promoted construction on a large scale in the regions around Cleveland, Sant'Antonio and Miami. Summoned by Nehru in 1945, he was put in charge of pilot projects in the rural areas of Uttar Pradesh, becoming Planning Advisor to the state government. Brought into the Chandigarh project in 1949, he came up with the first idea of a superblock, which although based on the neighborhood units of the band town, allowed the city to grow to a larger size.

Their involvement in the protocol for Indian towns helped to train figures like Charles Correa, [14] Raj Rewal, Balkrishna Doshi, A.G. Krishna Menon, P.L. Varma and Julius Vaz. [15]
As we have already seen, these were the architects who played a key role in the definition of a modern aesthetics suited to India and the development of an autonomous and differentiated language that led to the formalization of a specific grammar of planning in countries where the conditions were similar to those in India: technological backwardness, extreme poverty, lack of training, low levels of education, poor healthcare, grave social inequality and scanty social mobility.

Tropicalism as Centrality
—

The complexity of the problems led to responses that were for the most part linked to a set of design practices lumped together under the label of tropical architecture. [16]
Together, Westerners and Indians discussed and defined spatial mechanisms to be implemented on a large scale, a process that entailed the more or less active involvement of the end users. The principles on which all the social and economic engineering of the urban settlements was based can be set out as a series of points that define a relationship between inhabited spaces and strategies for getting the inhabitants to participate in the process of construction.

1. House—neighborhood unit—incrementalism. The starting point was the idea of the housing unit as a principle of equitable distribution of resources and reallocation of families in improved situations. The house, if possible detached, single story and necessarily with a space outdoors, unequivocally brought with it the idea of settlements of low and medium density in keeping with the paradigm of the garden city.

....

2. Districts—social diversity—time: the districts were planned to house different types of family and their respective wealth was marked by a greater availability of space, while the typological models remained the same. The arrangement of the different housing units depended on their position with respect to the road, services and public open space. The models could be built and handed over complete or partially constructed, especially in the service parts, and finished later by their occupants. The size and location of schools depended on their accessibility on foot, allowing women and children to move independently.

....

3. Roads—infrastructure—use: roads first of all, but infrastructure in general, were built according to a hierarchy of use, intended to keep the costs of construction to a minimum. The towns were served on a regional scale by a railroad or a bus station for mass transport; the main roads of connection and circulation were wide and paved with asphalt, while roads used for small-scale transport of goods and circulation were of medium size and unpaved, with broad open ditches for drainage; the secondary roads of access to the housing districts were asphalted, while small roads of circulation were unpaved. The sewage system was mixed, in part below ground and in part open, and a drainage system was provided for filtered runoff waters.

....

4. Public services—accessibility: all the structures for support and participation in daily life were located inside the districts: small-scale food retailers, post office, primary and secondary schools, small public libraries, social and health services and the local police station had to be at a distance that could be covered on foot by a 6-year-old child in a maximum of 15 minutes.

....

5. Institutional buildings—representation: administrative centers, theaters, museums and movie houses were located at the points of access to the residential districts and at the junctions of the main roads so that they could be reached as easily as possible.

....

6. Public space and parkland—public space and parks and gardens for leisure constituted an all-pervading means of traversing and connecting residential areas. They also provided a privileged corridor of access to open space and the surrounding countryside, with the aim of making possible a constant and fluid relationship with the fields and allowing the cultivation of vegetable gardens for a subsistence economy.

....

The architects who worked on the formulation of these principles, as a sustainable system that could be put into effect in depressed contexts, were the same ones who in the following years would set up the first departments of Tropical Studies at British universities, including Imperial College, the AA and the UCL, and put together the development and cooperation projects of the London School of Economics. And they were the same ones who, from the 1950s onward, became advisers to the United Nations and who helped to found UN-Habitat in 1975, establishing in a definitive manner the standards for a set of shared practices that were exported all over the world.

Otto Koenigsberger first went from Asia to Africa in 1956 to give his professional advice in Ghana and then again in 1964 to draw up the large-scale project for the urban area of Lagos. And his lectures and advice on bringing improvements to the so-called tropical countries, from South America to the Middle East, were innumerable, earning him the UN-Habitat Scroll of Honor in 1989. But all the others contributed to the spread of models of participatory development through university teaching and international projects. So the second half of the 20th century saw the emergence of a widely shared appreciation for practices like self-improvement and empowerment and incremental architecture, as well as for the implementation of specific expertise through the construction of new settlements, for the upgrading of skills through the

construction of buildings, for the definition of identities through research into historical forms and sharable common spaces, for the self-determination of communities through the regeneration of degraded areas or informal spaces, for the birth of new sectors of production through the use of low-cost and low-impact technologies and for the promotion of a new productivity through customization of the product made by local labor. [17]

What we are faced with here is a changed reality and the possibility of "Learning from India" or "Exporting India."

A New Modern and Processual Paradigm
–

How far today, however, should we distance ourselves from the Modern Movement? In other words, what can be retained and what should be eliminated in the definition of a paradigm of tropical modernity? In addition to egalitarianism and homogenization I believe it is necessary to single out sustainability and the attention to the natural environment.

Taken as a whole, in fact, these reflections make one thing in particular stand out: modernity and the "champions of the new architecture" bound a spatial system inseparably to the people who were going to live in it. In the majority of cases the land and the buildings remained public property or were owned by the cooperatives that were partners in the project. The social classes that the planners had in mind were principally that of the workers in the industries involved in the development of the areas and that of the public administrators of the towns and cities; in addition, the project took into consideration a lower middle class of traders who aimed to live off local commerce. Their disciples, the contemporary architects influenced to a greater or lesser extent by this global exchange of ideas, have often focused exclusively on the most deprived segments of the population, [18] who have crowded in surprising numbers around the cities, exerting a wholly unexpected social and demographic pressure and making an incalculable impact on them. The result has been an interest in participatory architecture on a minute scale, often self-built with local materials like bamboo and rammed earth or using mixed technology and labor trained on site.

Others, however, have fallen back on a refined and elitist modernist aesthetic still aimed at a cultured middle class, which on the whole shares the values of modernity but has no interest in a change of direction at the global scale. The considerations I am presenting here have become the motive for a revival of a common reflection on subjects that can reinstate the principles of modernity so closely bound up with the redistribution of basic rights. For these reasons I am trying to define a possible approach through the study and comparison of architects who were trained and have operated in regions of the tropical belt, united by the need to tackle similar problems, in a climate of crisis and urgency due to the new migratory pressure on established urban areas. [19]

I think the local problems emerging in countries that have specific circumstances like liberation from colonialism or dictatorship in common can be interpreted from the viewpoint of the establishment of a route to democratic government and a sharing of rights and duties. In architecture and city planning it is in fact possible to compare the experiences of those who in different ways and to different extents have had to deal with similar complexities in the effort to develop a new participatory modernity for the territory. There are architects who in their everyday activities continue to experiment with themes like incremental construction, the insertion of infrastructure and public space into spontaneous settlements, the temporary housing of families and provision of health facilities and the development of practical and soft techniques of building. I ask myself how these practices, devices and tools, normally utilized for small centers and communities, can instead be applied on a large scale and in much bigger areas, bringing changes that will result in a new shared aesthetics that I like to define as "processual." We know in fact that in India the period of reflection on adaptation and the activation of collective processes has not come to an end. On the contrary, the Indian cultural elite is developing, in various fields linked to urban planning, an original and innovative vision. I will give here the names of some of the principal exponents by way of example: the anthropologist Arjun Appadurai, who has coined the term "modernity at large" in relation to the emergence of a indigenized version; the architect Rahul Mehrotra, who with his research project Kinetic City has begun to carry out a study of temporary adaptability in Indian public space; the philosopher Parimal Patil, whose research is focused on the aesthetics and language of religion in Southeast Asia; the Bangladeshi economist Muhammad Yunus, who pioneered the concept of microcredit; the planners Anuradha Mathur and Dilip da Cunha, engaged in the definition of an environmentally friendly urbanism, attentive to variations in the climate. Their active participation in the international debate makes their contributions particularly relevant to the contemporary view of the relationship between modernity and the cultural heritage of the past. [20]

Tropicalism Is Participatory Modernity

The themes that are being widely tackled but still lack a complete and comprehensive overview are in fact the following:

1. The houses of delocalized production. Social and functional layering in settlements.

2. Various degrees of infrastructure from hardware to software. Infra-free systems, global interconnection and local networks.

3. The aesthetics of representation at different scales, up to those of pervasive accessibility for citizens to public institutions and the recognition of fundamental rights.

4. The implementation of a soft technology and self-building, including the use of local and sustainable materials on an urban and regional scale.

5. The recycling of resources and boosting the effectiveness of the local workers to increase the sustainability of the production cycle, including maintenance and dismantling.

6. Secular space for the coexistence of private spheres, and inclusive therefore of religious tolerance, different ethnic groups living in the same location, recognition of nationality and social diversity.

This set of practices, which appear to be

strategic, almost political indications, presupposes on the contrary an idea of the active and even practical participation of the people for whom the urban transformations or new living spaces are intended. Today it is a matter of understanding what kind of participation is possible and within what limits we need to keep the undeniable advantages of processual aesthetics if we are not going to lose the culture of space and of architectural design, the qualities that set space free from its ties to a specific time and use and consign it to the future, whatever that may be. This is in fact the aesthetics of the history of architecture: an aesthetics that is attributed on the one hand to monuments, but on the other and above all to the kind of architecture widespread in European cities. The architecture of beautiful squares, of streets. The spontaneous, anonymous architecture, that of the urban fabric in other words, the sort described by Camillo Sitte when he tried to give indications about how the city ought to be designed, by which he meant how its public space should be designed; but in addition to this properly and exclusively urban architecture, more in general the anonymous architecture to be found in historic human settlements, the sort studied by Giuseppe Pagano · [21] when he investigated the roots of modernity in Italy. The kind that was also presented as essential in the Mediterranean and sketched over and over again by Le Corbusier in his travel diaries. Later, this same architecture was recognized to have an aesthetic value of its own, linked to its processuality, to its occasional nature and variability over time. It is assigned the unique value of being the outcome of a shared and superhistorical activity. So the city, as a collective work, is the fruit of the active participation of the inhabitants who made it so magnificent and gave to it their wealth in exchange for security in the future and in the name of a sharing of the work that guaranteed them a greater wellbeing. This is why the city-states typical of the Italian peninsula are so diverse and so closely tied to the lands that grew and prospered around them under the political protection that they offered.

In fact a shared awareness has emerged with regard to the urban question: people have to be included in planning processes. As I have already pointed out · [22], it is only through architecture that communities organize themselves and plan for the future. Only the design of a new spatial configuration makes possible the public choice of goals and facilitates the control of expenditure and the management of material resources for construction, putting participation in democracy into effect. · [23] This is the de facto difference between the urban settlements that are considered parts of the city and the others, the slums. In architecture a sort of free thinking has been brought into play that puts the city back at the center and considers open and shared public space the keystone of ideas about the growth of the city of social rights. The community and the individual are its existential linchpin. Only expert design on the part of architects is able to inscribe the new processes in history, as it always refers, more or less consciously, to the history of human beings. An imaginative and visionary engagement is in fact the only one able to migrate, grafting on a deep change in thinking that puts the architecture of places back at the center of the debate over productive strategies of development, through the care taken over space and the use of it and its resources by the inhabitants. A debate that at the moment has run aground on the technological heights that seem to be able to tame climates and nature, but whose collective costs have always made people less free.

This had been clearly understood by the promoters of the first global world, who in fact drew on a technology that aimed to have a low impact, and it is still understood by those who commit themselves to a sustainable architecture in sustainable cities. A commitment rooted in the simple equation that architecture is made for human beings and should be within their grasp, from production to disposal. And that places at the center the principle of negotiation for a conscious modernity in the communities and societies in which they operate.

Warm Modernity
–

Starting out from the scale of architecture, · [24] we can define a possible future for the global city by embarking on a profound reappraisal of the urban model and of strategies of development and their impact. For urban life in itself and the city as a form of thought have been inseparably bound up with the idea of democracy, of participation in change, of control of the relationship between nation and population, which in our day has become a one-to-one relationship between state and citizenry. The modern secular space has not ceased to embody the participation and active involvement of the community in political debate. On the contrary it has been reactivated by its new electronic infrastructure, as was evident in the organization of the Arab Spring. It should not be forgotten, however, that in Africa the modern city has also meant racial segregation, gated communities and control of the lower classes, and the global city has signified technological differentiation and dramatization of inequalities in opposition to the principles of a participatory democracy. So the expertise of architects needs to be brought in first of all to stimulate an active debate, aimed at defining new approaches and the sharing of a processual aesthetics as paradigm of a new conscious and participatory modernity.

I think that the possibility of implementing a participatory project relies in the first place on the adaptation of an urban paradigm based on the design of the ground that guarantees the environmental and infrastructural connection, and that this can be used to trigger strategies for activation of the community whose character varies in relation to the cases and to the stage that the process of construction has reached.

As is clear from the case studies cited and the examples given, it is not in fact possible to determine in advance a single mode of participation of the people and the inhabitants involved. It has instead to be varied, adapted and negotiated. In history in fact we see that there are aspects in the process of realization of a city or its parts that concern its planning, others that regard the sharing of skills and capacities, still others that have to do with the development of a suitable technology, or with construction; and finally there are the ones that are related to everyday life, both of those who do the work and of those who will live in the places.

To speak of participation in an abstract sense today is in my view fairly reductive and does not take into account the real complexity of the process of construction of a city. [25] We know for example of the great failure of the ambitious plan for Brasilia due to collective amnesia over the need to provide accommodation for workers not only at the time of the city's construction, but also and above all after its birth: when it was inaugurated thousands of people came to take part in the celebrations and found themselves in a ghost town, devoid of life, on whose margins spontaneous and granular conglomerations were already springing up: the favelas of the workers, teeming with their own life and creating their own order. In spite of everything it is precisely the involvement of the parts that renders the birth of the city efficient and effective: not just the visionary ideas of dreamers, but also the opportunism of adventurers. Thus whatever the nature of the places we inhabit it is necessary for us to set about planning them in accordance with an ancient architectural idea: the one that ever since Vitruvius has compared buildings to a body whose limbs have to coexist in harmony. In my opinion a disciplinary version of this necessary approach to architectural design is needed for the city. It is for this reason that we have looked at the paradigm of the band town as the germ of a new awareness of planning. A shared maturation of this consideration attracts, in fact, planners active in that tropical but no longer marginal world that is giving signals of a profound change in the handling of space; planners engaged in a practice and a profession that take on structural problems, looking at that change with new faith. These men and women are not just architects and urbanists, but NGO development worker and information technologists, politicians and physicians, often figures cutting across professional boundaries who have grasped the importance of space and its infrastructures to the redistribution of wealth and who consider places to be the measure of the distance between heaven and earth: in short, utopia of living not just earthly riches.

NOTES

* 1

R. Riboldazzi, *La costruzione della città moderna*, which contains selected publications by the IFHTP from 1923 and 1938 (Milan: Jaca Book, 2010). R. Riboldazzi, *Un'altra Modernità. L'IFHTP e la cultura urbanistica.*

* 2

Ernst May (1886-1970) was city architect and planner in Frankfurt from 1925 to 1930. During these years he drew up the City Plan and designed and built numerous housing projects, including the Römerstadt and Westhausen Siedlungen. In the same years he edited the magazine *Zeitschrift das Neue Frankfurt*. In 1930 he moved to Moscow where he worked on the plan for expansion of the city in 1932 and on the founding of new industrial cities. In 1933 he went to work in Africa, traveling to Mombasa and settling in Tanzania. From 1945 onward he worked in Kampala and Nairobi.

* 3

H.-J. Henket and H. Heynen, *Back from Utopia* (Rotterdam: 010 Publishers, 2002).

* 4

On December 10, 1948, in Paris the United Nations General Assembly adopted the Universal Declaration of Human Rights, to be applied in all member states. It was drawn up in five languages, Chinese, French, English, Spanish and Russian. On December 14, 1960, the UN approved by a large majority a declaration condemning colonialism in all its forms. That year would go down in history as the Year of the Africa, with 17 states obtaining their independence. In 1966, when decolonization was almost complete, the International Covenant on Economic, Social and Cultural Rights and the International Covenant on Civil and Political Rights were approved by the UN. The principles expressed in these three documents formed the basis for all the projects of cooperation and development promoted by the United Nations in the countries in transition. Art. 1 of the Universal Declaration of Human Rights states: "All human beings are born free and equal in dignity and rights. They are endowed with reason and conscience and should act towards one another in a spirit of brotherhood."

* 5

Otto Koenigsberger (1908-99) was trained at the Technical University in Berlin and in 1933 he was hired by Ernst May's studio. Later, fleeing Nazism, he spent a short period in Egypt, where he began to carry out research into the adaptation of modern architecture to a different climate. In 1939 he moved to Mysore in India, where he had been appointed Chief Architect and Planner. In 1947 he was called on by Nehru to draw up the New Towns Protocol and run the Federal Housing and Planning Department, a post he would hold until 1951. From 1951 to 1954, in London, he set up the Department of Tropical Architecture at the Architectural Association, of which he was director until 1971. In 1978 he founded the Planning Unit at University College in London, which he ran until 1988. He worked with Charles Abrams for the UN missions on housing in developing countries in Ghana (1956), Pakistan (1957), the Philippines (1959 and 1978), Singapore (1963), Zambia (1964), Nigeria (1964), Ceylon (1966), Brazil (1968) and Malaysia (1970).

* 6

Tropicalismo was a cultural movement that developed in Brazil in the fifties and sixties. It is chiefly associated with music, but can very well be used as a metaphor for aspects linked to any form of artistic expression and thus to architecture as well. The music was the product of a complex alchemy of different forms, such as bossa nova, African music and fado, mixed up with rock, folk and jazz. Out of this came a sound that was an expression of a multicultural sensibility, based on the adaptation of ancient strains of music linked to the great diasporas and migrations resulting from colonial history.

* 7

The founding of Lúcio Costa's Brasília (1960) and Niemeyer's works of architecture reflected the desire of Juscelino Kubitschek's new democratic government to come up with new and original symbols.

* 8

The foundations of the Non-Aligned Movement were laid at the Bandung Conference of Asian and African States in 1955, as early as 1956 began officially a sensitization process for the involvement of countries with the same kind of problems and it was put on a formal footing in 1961.

* 9

In 1955, at the Bandung Conference, the economist Alfred Sauvy (1898-1990) defined the free-market system of the democratic and capitalist countries of the West as the First World, the economy of the communist and socialist countries allied with the Soviet Union as the Second World and that of the then developing countries, mostly former colonies in search of a sociopolitical identity and an economic policy of their own, as the Third World.

* 10

It should be remembered that Gandhi went to work in South Africa where he personally experienced the racial prejudice that underpinned the Apartheid System. Following his reading of John Ruskin's Unto This Last, he founded his first ashram, the Phoenix Settlement near Durban, in 1904, where members of the community farmed the land and practiced poverty and prayer, sharing the heavy work between them.

* 11

R. Mehrotra, A.J. Agarwal and S. Ganguly, Nehru, *Man among Men* (Delhi: R.M. Mital, 1990).

* 12

J. Drew and M. Fry, with H.L. Ford, *Village Housing in the Tropics* (London: Lund Humphries, 1947).

* 13

Jaspreet Takhar (ed.), *Celebrating Chandigarh: 50 Years of the Idea* (Ahmedabad: Maplin, 2002).

14

C. Correa, *Housing and Urbanisation* (London: Thames & Hudson, 1999)

* 15

R. Mehrotra, *Architecture in India since 1990* (Mumbai: Pictor Publishing, 2011).

* 16

O. Koenigsberger, T.G. Ingersoll, A. Mayhew and S.V. Szokolay, *Manual of Tropical Housing and Building* (London: Longman, 1974).

* 17

Self-improvement, in particular, takes place de facto in straitened circumstances and was adopted by UN-Habitat for its site and service protocols, but in architecture was part of the work and aesthetic research of Doshi, Rewal and Correa.

* 18

Think Global, Build Social!, exhibition staged at the Deutsches Architekturmuseum in Frankfurt in collaboration with ARCH+, June 7 - September 1, 2013.

* 19

Henket and Heynen, *Back from Utopia*, 2002.

* 20

M. Mostafavi and G. Doherty (eds), *Ecological Urbanism* (Baden: Lars Müller, 2010).

* 21

M. d'Alfonso, "Construir com imàgenes, construir – Building with images, building for real", G. Pagano, *Vocabulario de Imàgenes.*

* 22

M. d'Alfonso, M. Nastasi, *La città sospesa: L'Aquila dopo il terremoto* (Barcelona: Actar, 2015).

* 23

I. de Solà-Morales, *Decifrare l'Architettura* (Turin: Allemandi, 2001).

* 24

T. Avermaete, S. Karakayali and M. von Osten, *Colonial Modern: Aesthetics of the Past, Rebellions for the Future* (London: Black Dog, 2009).

* 25

D. Grahame Shane, *Urban Design Since 1945: A Global Perspective* (New York: John Wiley, 2012).

a further dialogue

/

MAPS BY ELISA FISCON

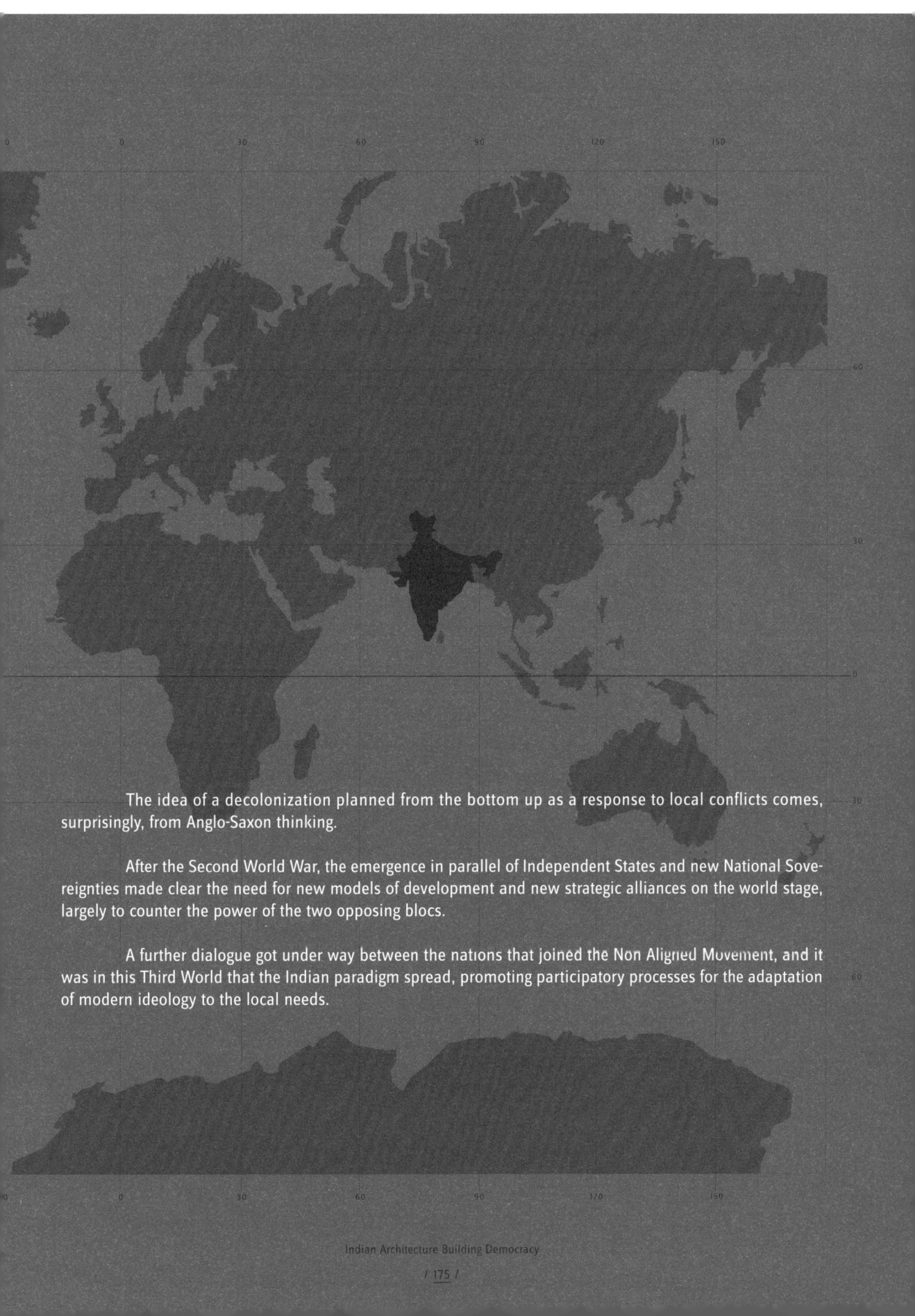

The idea of a decolonization planned from the bottom up as a response to local conflicts comes, surprisingly, from Anglo-Saxon thinking.

After the Second World War, the emergence in parallel of Independent States and new National Sovereignties made clear the need for new models of development and new strategic alliances on the world stage, largely to counter the power of the two opposing blocs.

A further dialogue got under way between the nations that joined the Non Aligned Movement, and it was in this Third World that the Indian paradigm spread, promoting participatory processes for the adaptation of modern ideology to the local needs.

COMMONWEALTH OF NATIONS

/

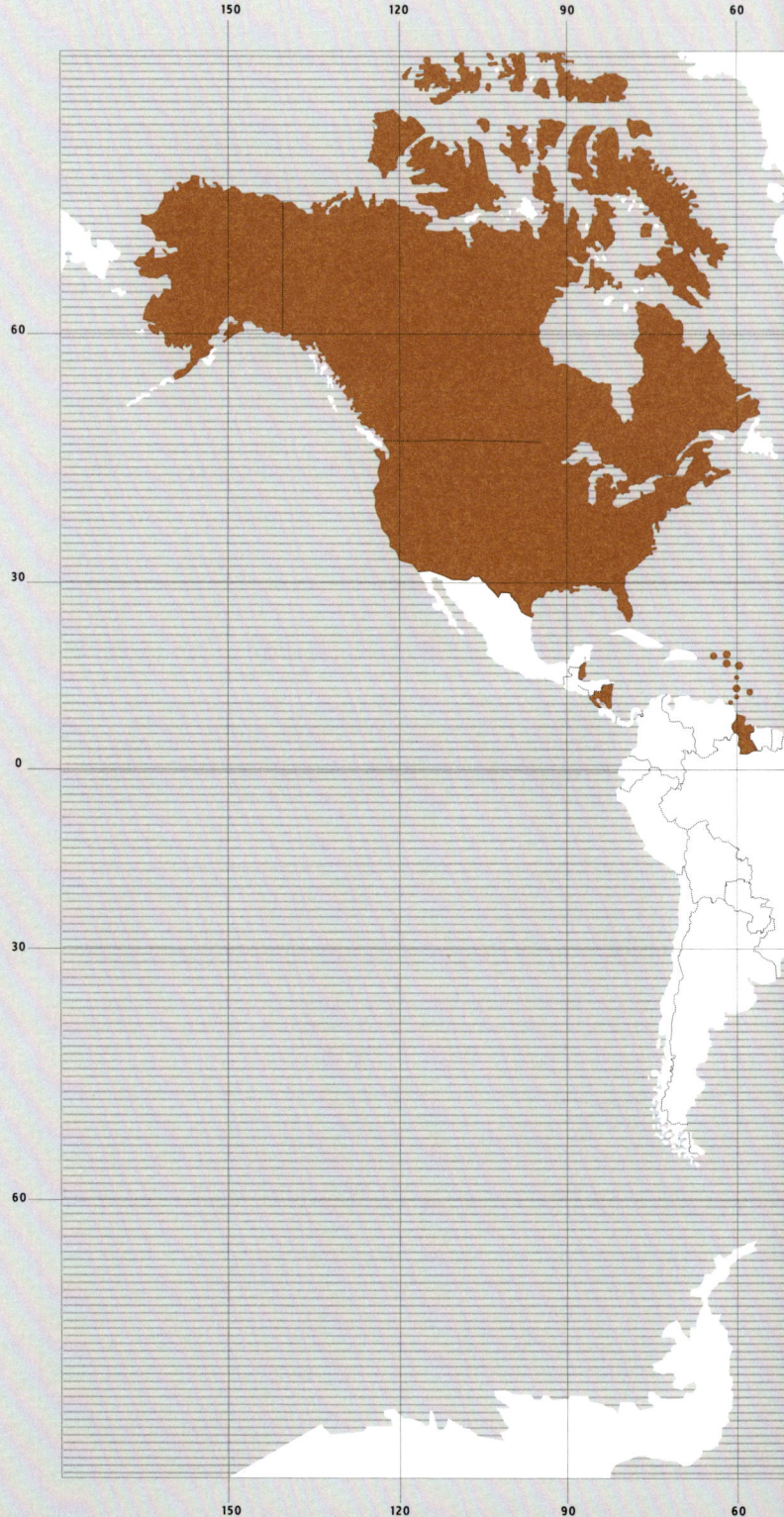 NATIONS

UNITED KINGDOM (1931)
CANADA (1931)
SOUTH AFRICA (1931; Released
in 1961 but returned in 1994
after the end of apartheid)
AUSTRALIA (1942; invited in 1931
but ratified in 1942)
NEW ZEALAND (1947; invited in
1931 but ratified in 1947)
INDIA (1947)
PAKISTAN (1947; released in 1972,
returned in 1989, suspended
in 2007)
SRI LANKA (1948)
GHANA (1957)
MALAYSIA (1957)
NIGERIA (1960; suspended in
1995 but readmitted in 1999)
CYPRUS (1961)
SIERRA LEONE (1961)
JAMAICA (1962)
TRINIDAD AND TOBAGO (1962)
UGANDA (1962)
KENYA (1963)
TANZANIA (1964)
MALAWI (1964)
MALTA (1964)
ZAMBIA (1964)
SINGAPORE (1965)
GUYANA (1966)
BOTSWANA (1966)
LESOTHO (1966)
BARBADOS (1966)
MAURITIUS (1968)
SWAZILAND (1968)
SAMOA (1970)
TONGA (1970)
FIJI (1970; output in 1987 returned
in 1997 suspended in 2006)
BANGLADESH (1972)
BAHAMAS (1973)
GRENADA (1974)
PAPUA NEW GUINEA (1975)
SEYCHELLES (1976)
SOLOMON ISLANDS (1978)
TUVALU (1978)
DOMINICA (1978)
SAINT LUCIA (1979)
SAINT VINCENT AND GRENADINE
(1979)
KIRIBATI (1979)
VANUATU (1980)
ANTIGUA & BARBUDA (1981)
BELIZE (1981)
MALDIVES (1982)
SAINT KITTS & NEVIS (1983)
BRUNEI (1984)
NAMIBIA (1990)
MOZAMBIQUE (1995)
CAMEROON (1995)
NAURU (1999)
RWANDA (2009)

Commonwealth realms
ANTIGUA & BARBUDA
AUSTRALIA
BAHAMAS
BARBADOS
BELIZE
CANADA
JAMAICA
GRENADA
SOLOMON ISLANDS
NEW ZEALAND
PAPUA NEW GUINEA
UNITED KINGDOM
SAINT KITTS AND NEVIS
SAINT VINCENT AND GRENADINE
SAINT LUCIA
TUVALU

Commonwealth Nations that have
their own monarchy
BRUNEI
LESOTHO
MALAYSIA
WAZILAND
TONGA

Republics of the Commonwealth
IRELAND
ZIMBABWE
GAMBIA
BANGLADESH
BOTSWANA
CAMEROON
CIPRO
DOMINICA
FIJI
GHANA
GUYANA
INDIA
KENYA
KIRIBATI
MALAWI
MALDIVES
MALTA
MAURITIUS
MOZAMBIQUE
NAMIBIA
NAURU
NIGERIA
PAKISTAN
RWANDA
SAMOA
SEYCHELLES
SIERRA LEONE
SINGAPORE
SRI LANKA
SOUTH AFRICA
TANZANIA
TRINIDAD AND TOBAGO
UGANDA
ZAMBIA

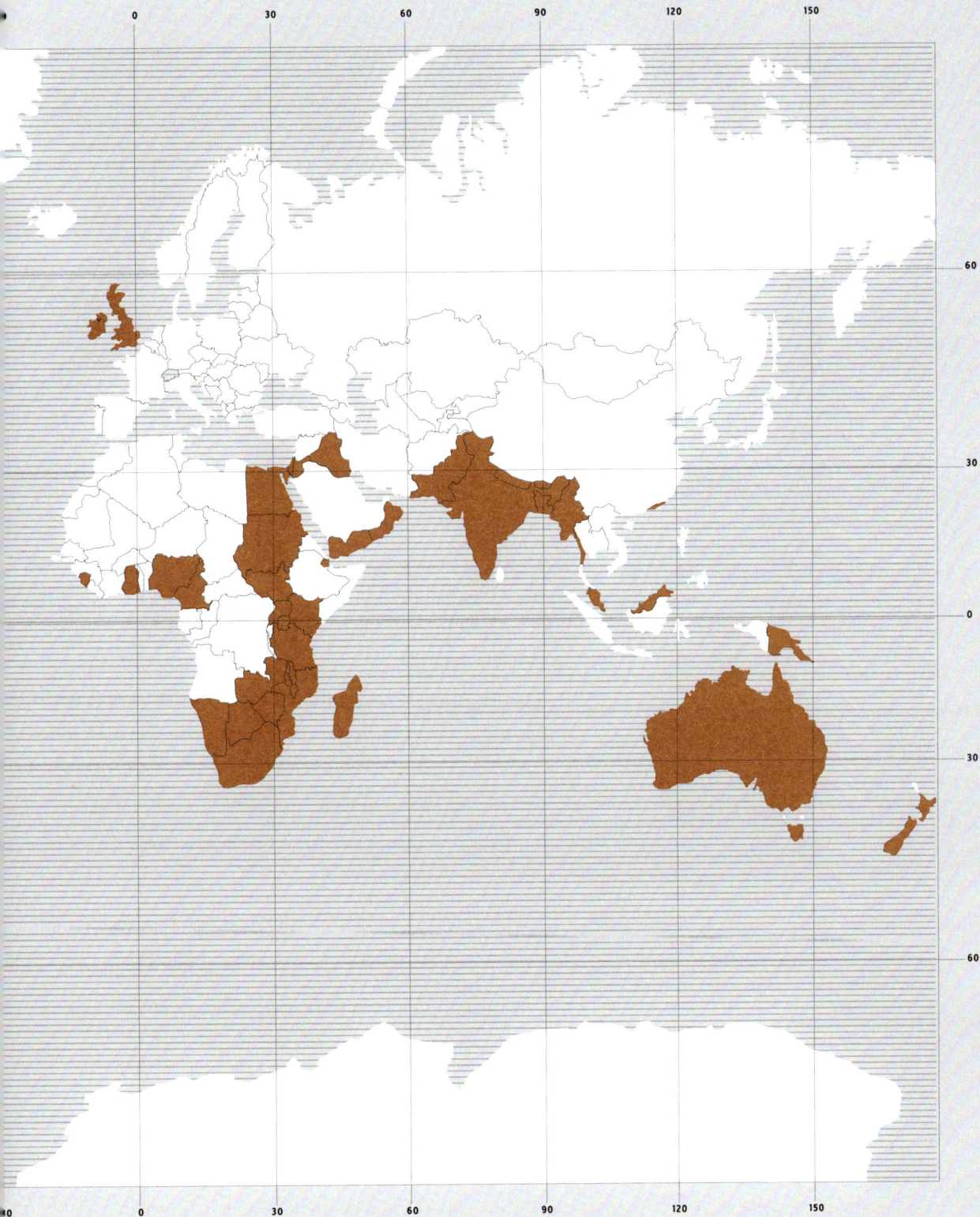

Indian Architecture Building Democracy

ONU
MEMBERS

/

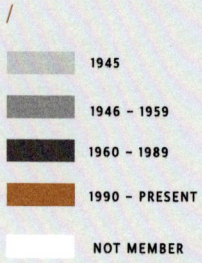

1945

1946 – 1959

1960 – 1989

1990 – PRESENT

NOT MEMBER

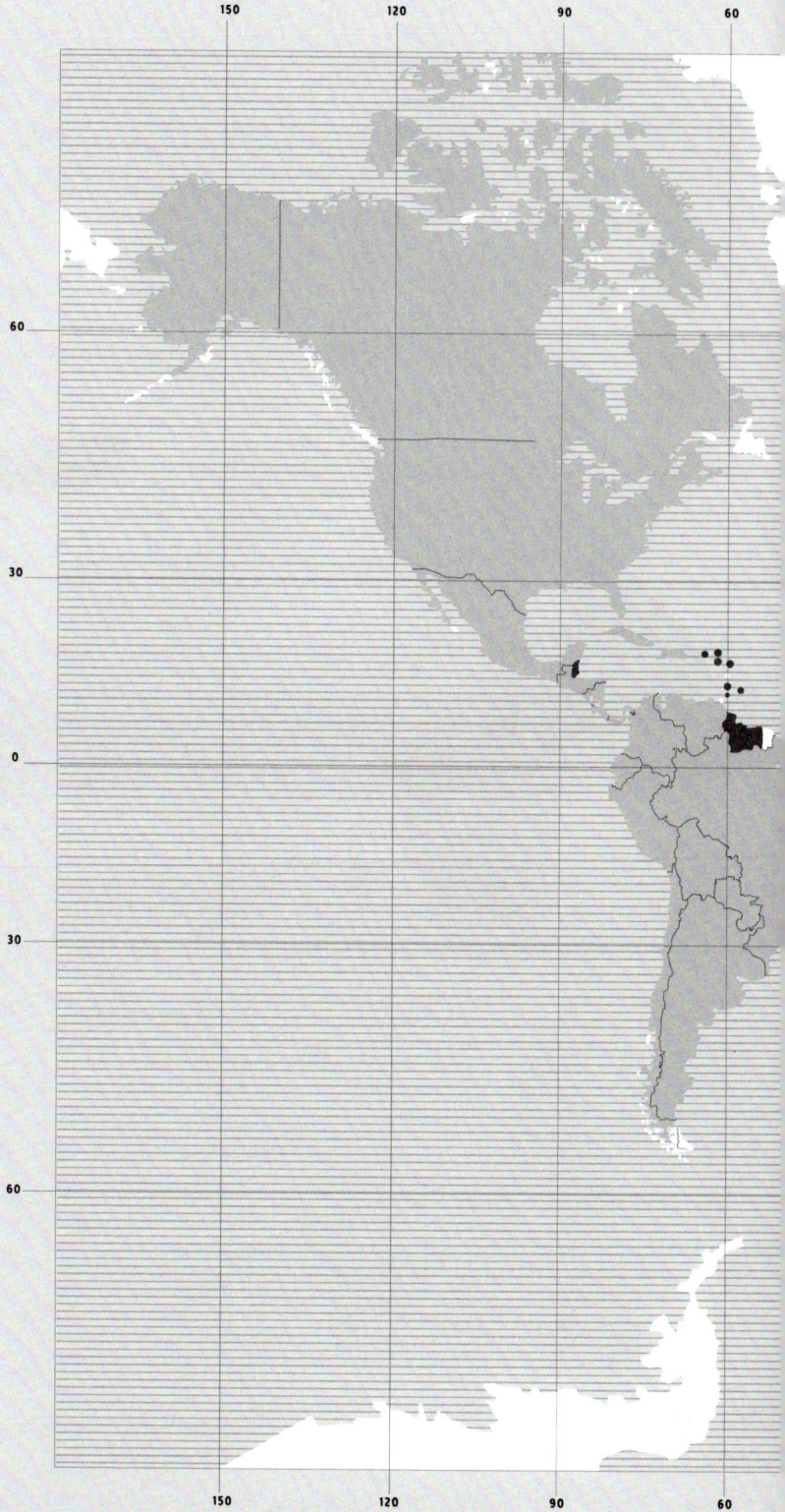

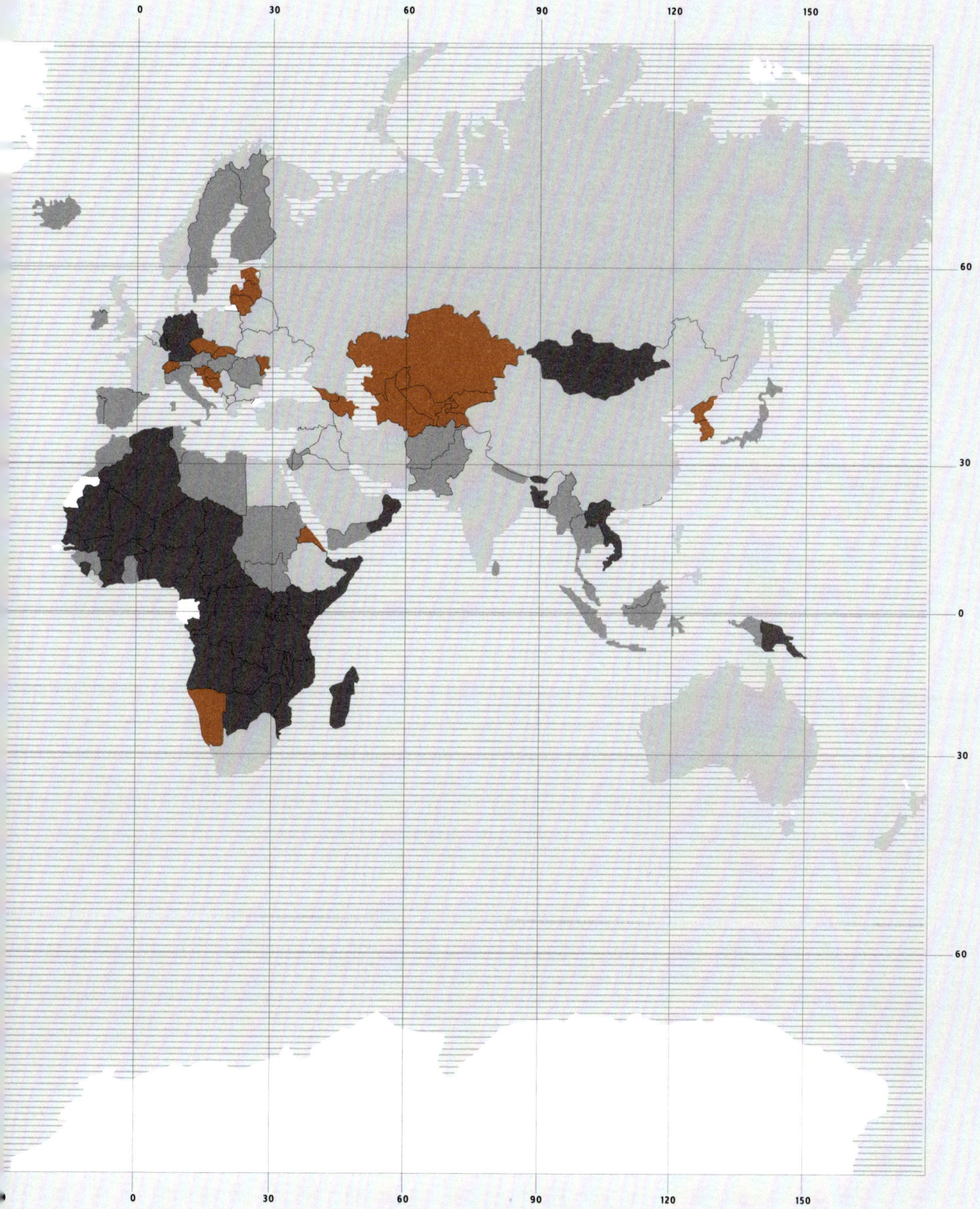

Indian Architecture Building Democracy

NOT ALIGNED
COUNTRIES

/

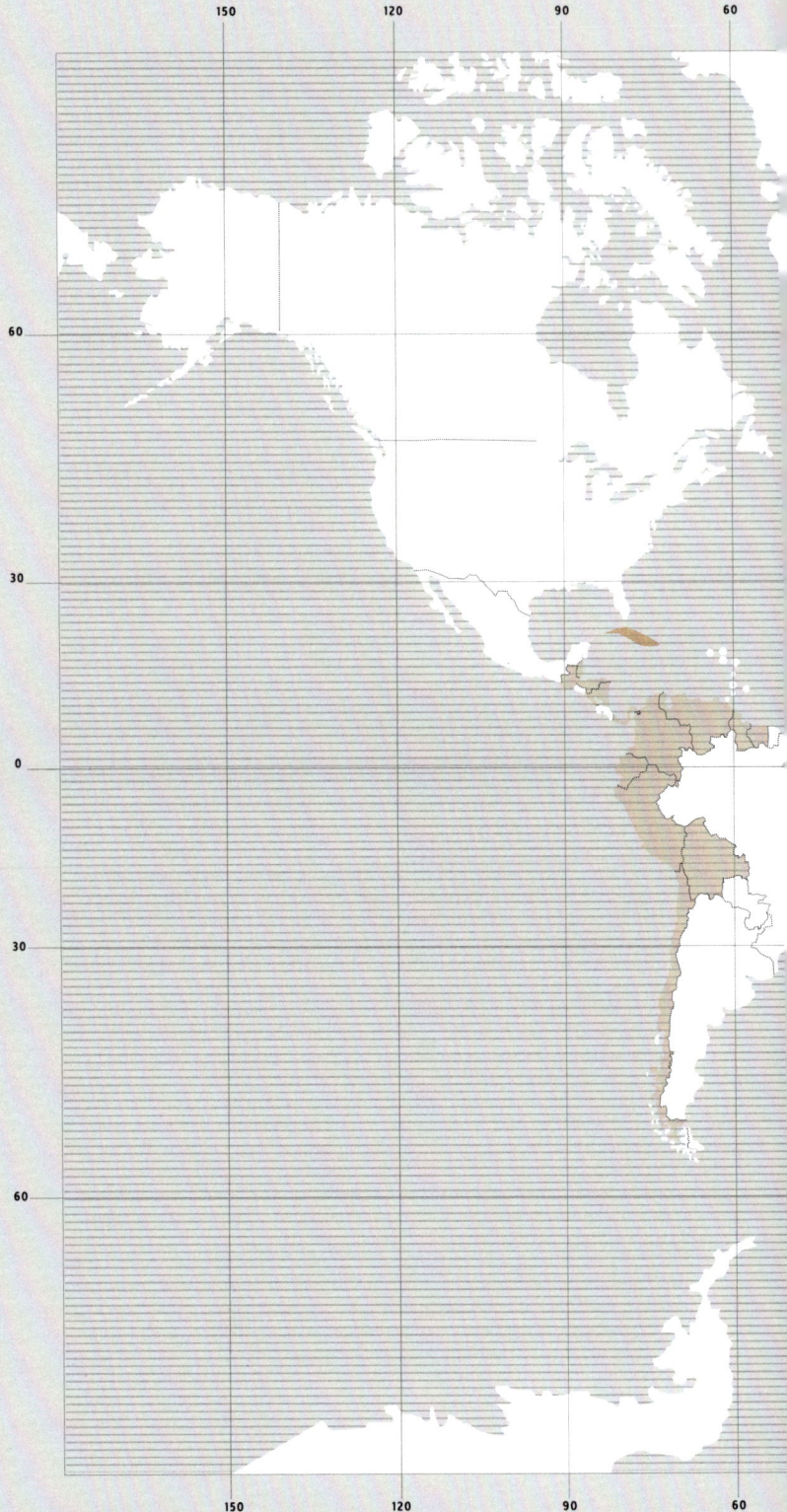

1955 – PARTICIPANT COUNTRIES
TO THE BANDUNG CONFERENCE

1961 – MEMBERS OF THE NON-ALIGNED
MOVEMENT AFTER THE CONFERENCE
OF BELGRADO

2012 – MEMBERS OF THE
NON-ALIGNED MOVEMENT

AFRICA
Currently every African country
is a member of the Non-Aligned
Movement.
AFGHANISTAN (1961)
ALGERIA (1961)
CAMBODIA (1961)
CUBA (1961)
D. R. OF CONGO (1961)
EGYPT (1961)
ETHIOPIA (1961)
GHANA (1961)
GUINEA (1961)
INDIA (1961)
INDONESIA (1961)
IRAQ (1961)
LEBANON (1961)
MALI (1961)
MOROCCO (1961)
MYANMAR (1961)
NEPAL (1961)
SAUDI ARABIA (1961)
SOMALIA (1961)
SRI LANKA (1961)
SUDAN (1961)
TUNISIA (1961)
YEMEN (1961)
ANGOLA (1964)
BENIN (1964)
BURUNDI (1964)
CAMEROON (1964)
CENTRAL AFRICAN R. (1964)
CHAD (1964)
JORDAN (1964)
KUWAIT (1964)
KENYA (1964)
LAOS (1964)
LIBERIA (1964)
LIBYA (1964)
MALAWI (1964)
MAURITANIA (1964)
NIGERIA (1964)
R. OF CONGO (1964)
SENEGAL (1964)
SIERRA LEONE (1964)
SYRIA (1964)
TANZANIA (1964)
TOGO (1964)
UGANDA (1964)
ZAMBIA (1964)
BOTSWANA (1970)
EQUATORIAL GUINEA (1970)
GABON (1970)
GUYANA (1970)
JAMAICA (1970)
LESOTHO (1970)
MALAYSIA (1970)
SINGAPORE (1970)
RWANDA (1970)
SWAZILAND (1970)
TRINIDAD & TOBAGO (1970)
U. ARAB EMIRATES (1970)
BANGLADESH (1973)

BURKINA FASO (1973)
BHUTAN (1973)
CHILE (1973)
CÔTE D'IVOIRE (1973)
MADAGASCAR (1973)
GAMBIA (1973)
MAURITIUS (1973)
NIGER (1973)
OMAN (1973)
PERU (1973)
QATAR (1973)
BELIZE (1976)
CAPE VERDE (1976)
GUINEA-BISSAU (1976)
COMOROS (1976)
MALDIVES (1976)
MOZAMBIQUE (1976)
NORTH KOREA (1976)
PANAMA (1976)
SÃO TOMÉ & PRÍNCIPE (1976)
SEYCHELLES (1976)
STATE OF PALESTINE (1976)
VIETNAM (1976)
BOLIVIA (1979)
GRENADA (1979)
IRAN (1979)
NAMIBIA (1979)
NICARAGUA (1979)
PAKISTAN (1979)
ZIMBABWE (1979)
BAHAMAS (1983)
BARBADOS (1983)
COLOMBIA (1983)
DJIBOUTI (1983)
ECUADOR (1983)
SAINT LUCIA (1983)
SURINAME (1983)
VANUATU (1983)
VENEZUELA (1989)
BRUNEI (1993)
GUATEMALA (1993)
MONGOLIA (1993)
PAPUA NEW GUINEA (1993)
PHILIPPINES (1993)
THAILAND (1993)
UZBEKISTAN (1993)
SOUTH AFRICA (1994)
ERITREA (1995)
HONDURAS (1995)
TURKMENISTAN (1995)
BELARUS (1998)
DOMINICAN REPUBLIC (2000)
EAST TIMOR (2003)
SAINT VINCENT AND THE GRENA-
DINES (2003)
ANTIGUA & BARBUDA (2006)
DOMINICA (2006)
HAITI (2006)
SAINT KITTS & NEVIS (2006)
AZERBAIJAN (2011)
FIJI (2011)

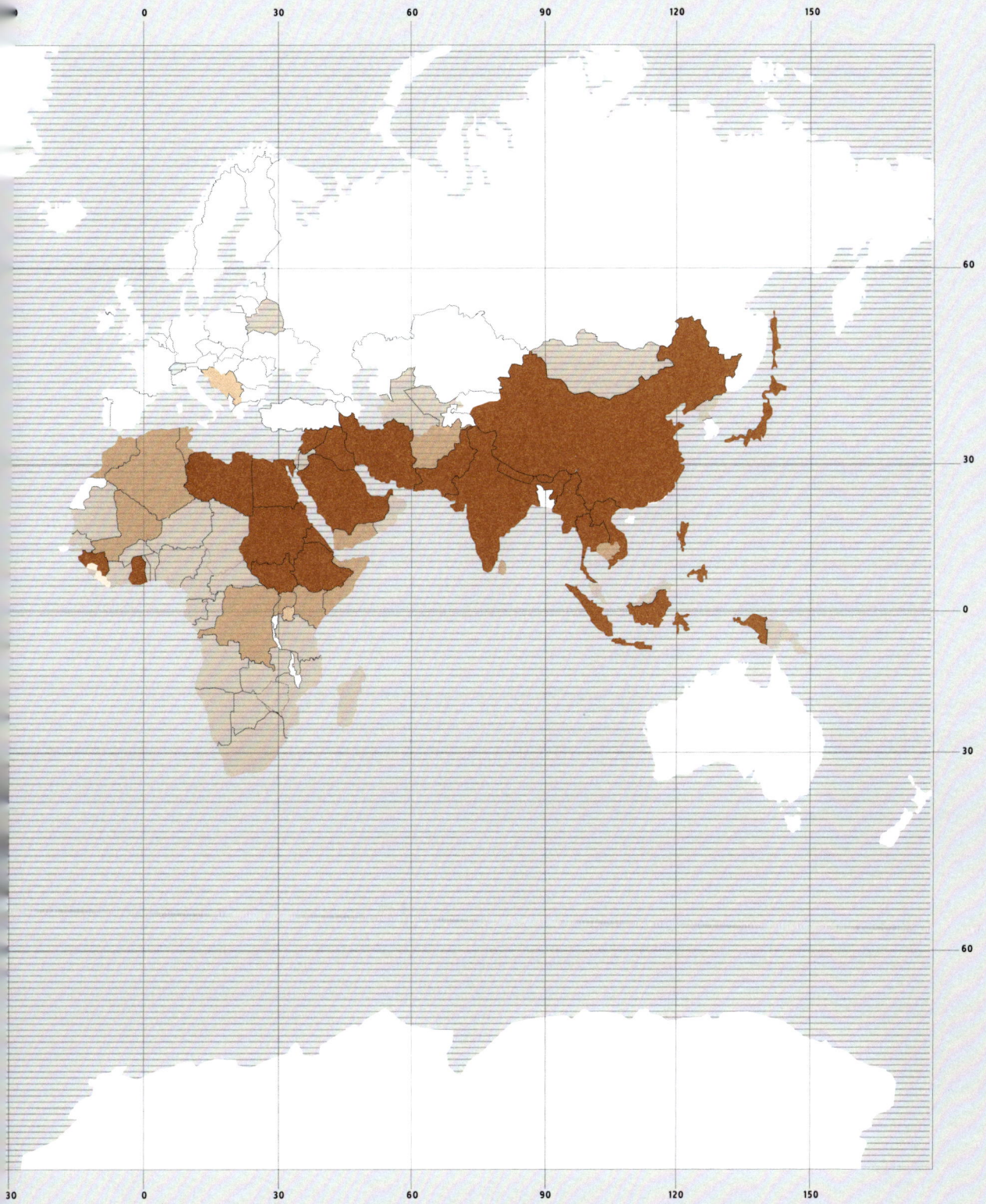

Indian Architecture Building Democracy

TROPICAL
BELT

/

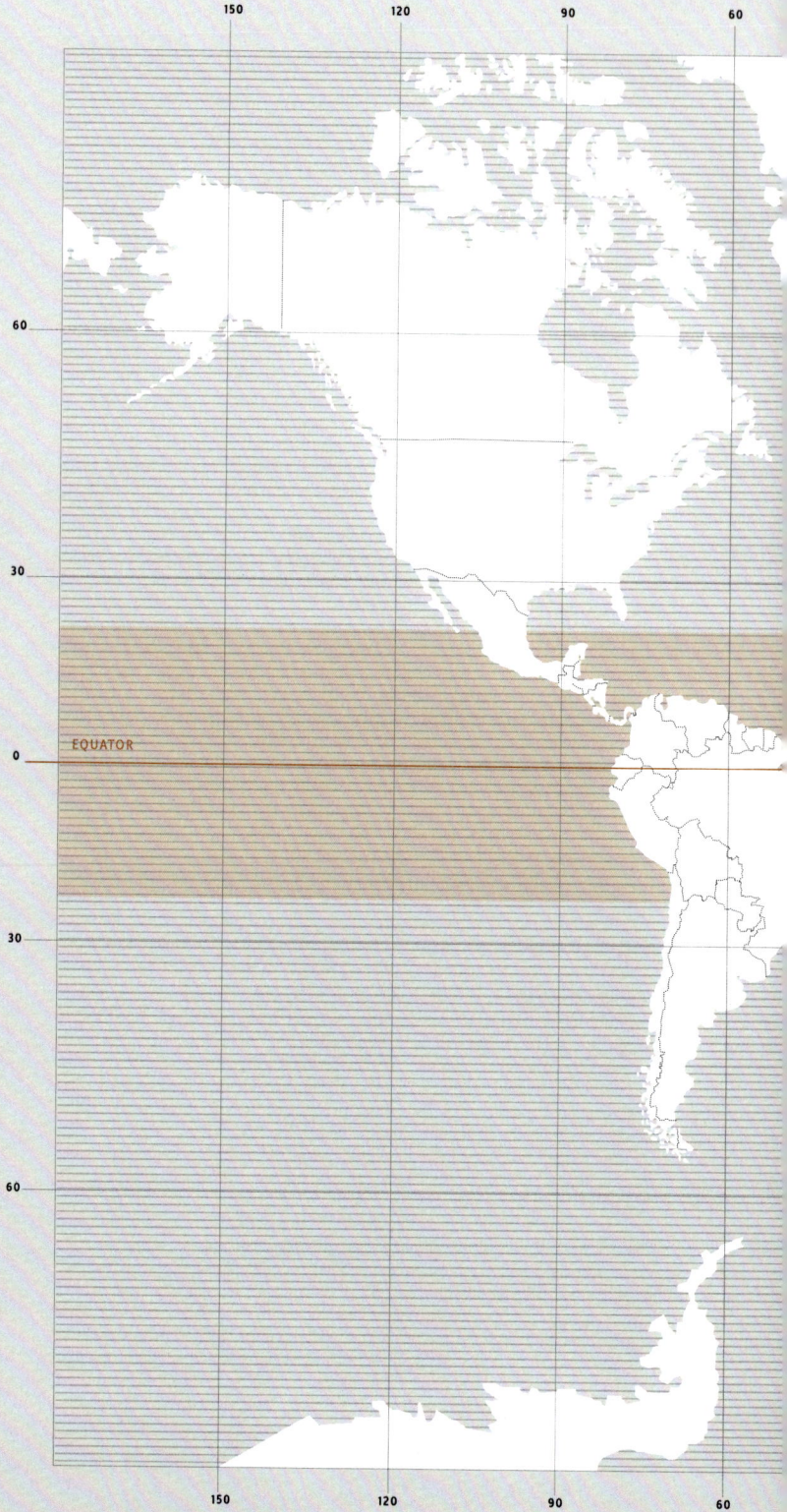
TROPICAL BELT

150   120   90   60

60

30

0   EQUATOR

30

60

150   120   90   60

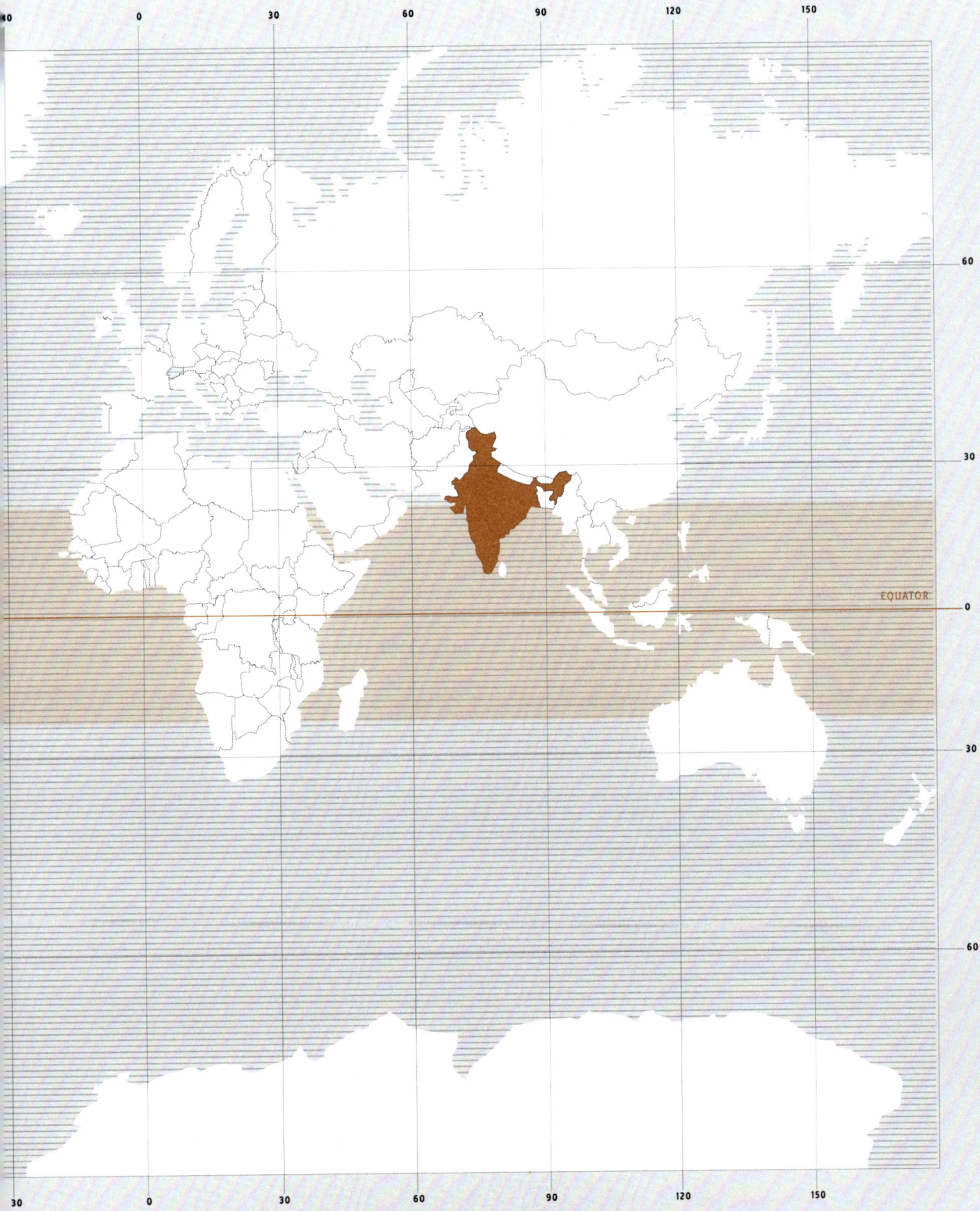

Indian Architecture Building Democracy

TOOLS OF PARTICIPATION. THE ROLE OF DESIGN MANUALS IN COLONIAL AND POSTCOLONIAL HISTORY

/

JACOPO GALLI

During his 50 years long career Edwin Maxwell Fry had the chance of working alongside many protagonists of the modern movement, two above all: Walter Gropius and Le Corbusier. Maxwell Fry hosted Gropius when he was fleeing from Germany and the nazi regime and was the project leader in the development of Chandigarh alongside Corbu. It is paradoxical to notice that while the highlight of Gropius' career was the establishment of an heroic creative school and Corbu's the establishment of his own figure as the head of the modern movement, Fry's higher achievement was not a building nor a urban scheme but the design manual *Tropical Architecture in the Dry and Humid Zones* [1] that he published with his wife Jane Drew in 1964. The manual partially challenges the general discourse on modern movement that has a global design language carried on by a rather small group of heroic masters and introduces the concept of modernity as a tool to fight the condition of underdevelopment of many parts of the word. The manual can be seen as a top down instrument capable of spreading knowledge from a small group of global experts to a large heterogeneous public as well as a tool for participation where a basic set of informations could be applied to specific conditions.

The manual attitude will highly influence the designs of development cooperators that can be considered in the bigger framework of the appropriate technology ideology, initiated by *Ghandi's Swadeshi* [2] movement and officially defined by Ernst "Fritz" Schumacher in his 1973 book *Small Is Beautiful.* [3] The movement advocated the use of bu-

ilding technologies suitable to the social and economic conditions of the geographic area in which they are to be applied while promoting self-sufficiency on the part of those using it. The movement was marginal in the European debate but central in African and Asian development works. The use of vaults or arches as well as of raw earth or recycled materials became an instrument to confront with local cultures, a sort of architectural Négritude that completely challenged the cosmopolitan vision of the tropics. The appropriate technology designs were often highly participative in their construction process but lacked the exemplifying capacity and the progressive cultural approach of Tropical Architecture.

Today, 50 years after the publication of Tropical Architecture and fully in the age of archistars, the manual approach still haunt us. The idea that the main goal of an architect is not to build a Babylon Tower but to provide a system of restrictions that enable participation is today most important then ever. Climate change and demographic processes have showed us that in many parts of the world the planned environment imagined by the modern masters, as well as the bottom up approach of the appropriate technology, are simply impossible. Architecture can still have a value only if able to propose open systems guided by strong cultural attitudes allowing different professional figures to participate in the design debate and in the building process. The attitude of the manual is still alive and can still be a guidance for the future, the idea that transnational experts can provide cosmopolitan ideas adaptable to different conditions is made stronger by the new means of communication. Internet in particular has allowed the public of manuals to virtually enlarge to the whole planet, and the open-source movement gave the intriguing but dangerous possibility to transform everyone in a global expert as well as in a possible participant to design experiments. The manual, with the obvious updates in means and forms, can still be a tool to propose a possible vision of modernity. A modernity that can find in the Third World a fertile testing ground establishing new forms and manners exportable at a global scale.

In the fields of construction design manuals trace back to the dawn of times · [4] but the emerging of global phenomenas, such as imperialism and worldwide commerce, gave new life to this literary category. Manuals and handbooks were not limited to the building sector: botanical handbooks, instructional manuals to collect ethnographic evidences, primers on farming and livestock cultivation and colonial housekeeping guides · [5] were all instruments for the efficient annexation, occupation and management of the colonies. The manual debate was carried on first by medical and hygiene experts and then by military engineers who standardized the prescriptions into a set of fixed rules linked to climatic parameters. It is hard to draw a clear line in the manual production regarding constructions since works range from Francis Galton's *The Art of Travel* · [6], a handbook for adventurers and explorers in extreme conditions, to Samuel Swinton Jacob's *Jeypore Portfolio* · [7], a precise reproduction of the refined architectural elements of the Indian Jaipur region.

The standardized method, was discarded only in the postwar years when colonial powers realized the incumbent independence of the colonies and implemented plans of *planned decolonization*. · [8] Europeans accepted the fact that in the upcoming years the magnitude and rhythm of transformations in Africa and in Asia would not allow them to fully control changes and tried to provide open tools able to enable locals to intervene directly. In 1947 Maxwell Fry published alongside his wife Jane Drew the pocket manual *Village Housing in the Tropics* that contained diagrammatic plans for houses, schools and community centers of blandly simple design with pitched roofs and strip windows. · [9] The

architectural approach was open to participation, modernity could be exported through a down-to-earth approach that provided simple technical tools to an unskilled population in order to optimize self-construction.

With the publication of the final version of *Tropical Architecture in the Dry and Humid Zones* in 1964 the discourse shifted to a completely different public, the book can be intended not merely as a manual but as a toolbox. It is a sum of tools that the author proposes to future designers, not fixed rules but qualitative devices that can be modified accordingly to climatic conditions and the architect's creativity. Fry&Drew realized that modernity could not simply conquer tropical regions bottom-up without the creation of a educated class able to comprehend and apply what was shifting from a technical issue to a cultural attitude. In the introduction of the book they stated: "We write [...] for the growing number of those who inhabit this regions [...]. On these architects and planners falls the major burden of creating an environment in which the tropical people may flourish. [...] So will the future architects who build for their own tropical people bring to their tasks, emotions, sympathies and knowledge denied to us who come from outside." · [10] This sentence clearly defines the public of the manual: a newborn cultural elite that, in the framework of a progressive world, could be able to guide the tropical world towards a modern future while at the same time protect and strengthen millennial traditional cultures.

The manual *Tropical Architecture* shows its debt to previous experiences in its structure but at the same time proposes a radically new approach. The manual ceases to be solely a technical instrument and becomes a cultural guide for participation, specifically thought for architects and planners. This approach could not be further away from the fully planned environment imagined by modern masters, the manual opens up a new field of modernity, a new territorialization of architecture not based on a single genius but on an experimental and scientific attitude where climate becomes the main shaper of architectural forms. As Nicholas Negroponte will affirm years later in *Soft Architecture Machines* architectural design "will not be a case of reckless autocracy, rather it would be a pervasive and evasive set of restrictions that would result from the good intentions of being comprehensive, orderly and empirically correct." [11]

The manual establishes a clear set of cultural and technical restrictions, having climatic data as an orderly starting point and opening up possibilities to designer willing to comprehend the approach and use the provided tools. With the manual Fry&Drew demonstrated their progressive and cosmopolitan view of the tropics: the underdeveloped world could be helped by technological and scientific tools open to participation. The success of the book pushed other professionals to draft their own manuals. Many of this authors were teacher or students in the Department of Tropical Architecture that opened in 1954 at the Architecture Association in London. The course was the first attempt to establish an institution in which the spirit of the manual could find an academic dimension. Geographically distant architects could meet in a neutral environment where they could absorb, comprehend, modify and disseminate a common cultural attitude: the cosmopolitan development of the world was possible!

The most important evolution in the manual discourse was provided by the monumental work of Otto Königsberger, *Manual of Tropical Housing and Building* [12] published in 1974 after more then 20 years of research on building materials and techniques. The manual diverges considerably from the structure, full of examples and imagines, of Fry&Drew's *Tropical Architecture*, Königsberger's manual is an ordered collection of computing systems with a technical approach: the tropical version of Ernst Neufert's *Architects' Data*. [13] Königsberger identified in technical solutions the main tool through which modernity could be exported in non-western environments. The spirit of cultural participation that permeated Fry&Drew's book was shifted towards building techniques adapted to tropical climatic conditions, the idea that modernity was not solely a technological problem but rather a cultural attitude that could be melted to local traditions was lost.

In the same years other protagonists emerged in the African and Asian scene: international organizations imagined development through eco-nomic and professional aid. The United Nations and UNESCO, addressed the problem for a long time period and through different means but failed to clearly institute a cultural and technical approach replicable in different conditions. The most important experimental field for development was education, the school building programs initiated at the end of the colonial period were picked up by the new independent nations alongside european cooperators. [14] The spirits of the design manuals was revisited with respect to the new social conditions and to the lower amount of public money. UNESCO in particular drafted guidelines and built prototypes giving attention to the indigenization of both teaching methods and design processes.

Today what's left of this multilayered experiences? Can the manual tradition find new life with new technological devices and communication systems? The path to walk is still long but the past provides us a solid cultural attitude: the capacity to comprehend architecture as a toolbox providing instruments for development and participation. A participation useful only if guided by strong concepts, set of restrictions not to be intended as limits but rather as possibilities.

NOTES

1

A first version of the book titled *Tropical Architecture in the Humid Zones* was published in 1956, due to editorial reasons instead of publishing only the remaining volume Fry&Drew decided to unify all their works in a single volume that was finally published in 1964. Iain Jackson, Jessica Holland, T*he Architecture of Edwin Maxwell Fry and Jane Drew*, (Franham: Ashgate, 2014).

2

S. Kumar, "Gandhi's Swadeshi - The Economics of Permanence", in J. Mander, E. Goldsmith, *The Case Against the Global Economy: And for a Turn Toward the Local* (San Francisco: Sierra Club Books, 1996).

3

E.F. Schumacher, *Small Is Beautiful: A Study of Economics as if People Mattered* (London: Blond & Briggs, 1973).

4

To some extents the works of Vitruvius or Leon Battista Alberti can be considered manuals as well as the personal and secret text produced by medieval masons.

5

I. Osayimwese, "Demystifying Colonial Settlement: Building Handbooks for Settlers in the German Colonies, 1904-1930", in V. Langbehn, *German Colonialism, Visual Culture, and Modern Memory* (London-New York: Routledge, 2010).

6

F. Galton, *The Art of Travel; Or, Shifts and Contrivances Available in Wild Countries* (London: John Murray, 1872).

7

V. Arora, *Samuel Swinton Jacob and the Jeypore Portfolio: issues in Architectural Recording* (Master dissertation at Bath University, 2009).

8

J. Flint, "Planned decolonization and its failure in British Africa", *African Affairs*, 328, 1983.

9

E. Mumford, *The CIAM discourse on Urbanism, 1928-1960* (Cambridge: MIT Press, 2002).

10

E. Maxwell Fry, J. Drew, *Tropical architecture in the dry and humid zones* (London: Reinhold Pub. Corp., 1964).

11

N. Negroponte, *Soft Architecture Machines* (Cambridge: MIT Press, 1975).

12

O. Königsberger, O.H. Ingersoll, T.G. Mayhew, *Manual of Tropical Housing & Building* (London: Longman, 1974).

13

E. Neufert, *Architects' Data* (London: Lockwood, 1936).

14

K. de Raedt, "Between 'true believers? And operational experts: UNESCO architects and school building in post colonial Africa", *The Journal of Architecture*, 19, 2014.

INDIGENOUS TECHNOLOGIES
AND SELF COSTRUCTION

/

INGRID PAOLETTI

Introduction
–

India is a complex changing, contradictory and fascinating mosaic, where the distance with the West is still, fortunately, sensitive. A different conception of architecture, based on historical references and settlement models stranger to us, on the importance of time as conforming agent, on the changing role of technology, on different conceptions of space, memory and place: these are some of the challenges posed today by a country that is not willing to uncritically absorb any new form of colonialism · [1]. The Indian climatic, historical, anthropological differences, due to the sum of very different cultures and religions, persist in architecture and its techniques, to reinforce the strangeness to historical movements that could somehow make it homogeneous in languages and results. Building technologies become in this context an opportunity for close comparison with the contest and the conditions in which they are used, not only as a tool to solve a spatial problem but with that 'social' connotation in some way, which strengthen the 'mentality' explained above.

Modernism and Contemporary Techniques
–

The first phase of Indian modernism includes roughly the period that can be inscribed within the state of Nehru (1947-1975), period in which modernism took a very strong symbolic value of confidence in the future. The techniques have been employed in a very similar manner to Western countries, with a propensity to use brick, which by its nature has a strong local presence. The "modern project" sees the East-West relationship constantly redefined and this experience of modernization seeks to re-establish an identity of a Nation that actually will never be prosecuted for cultural and climatic diversity—already outlined earlier in the text—, although inspired by those socialist ideals that will influence the future democratic India.

The physical infrastructure seek to bring also a social infrastructure through the regulation of space and the use of techniques that convey to regular geometries, trying to adapt to a very diverse and powerfully natural environment like India. What has characterized India has been the phenomenon of a simultaneous acceptance and resistance to Western ideologies. Modernism was in fact been seen as an attempt to merge Western forms with local issues, using the ideas and lessons from the past with contemporary materials and techniques.

The independence of India and its second Modernism, although apparently sanctioned the closure of the debate on architecture and identity, in reality it has not produced the society for which the country had hoped and desired, finding instead at the end a fragmented society inherited by the Nation. At the same time, a bigger attention to tradition lead to attempts to revive traditional crafts to solve problems either of cultural identity either of economic adequacy. The multi-ethnic and multi-religious society finds today a heritage to refer to linked on the one hand to ideological modernism slightly rooted in the context, on the other hand to a handicraft production that persists and indeed has perhaps the greatest potential for development in a current perspective. We can think at ceramics technologies and those of clay, dried handcrafted brick and bamboo as a finishing element or sometimes as a structural element. Reconciling these craftsmanship production methods with modernist principles of certainty and predictable rigor, has been difficult and has required a strong linguistic taming which reflects the kaleidoscopic pluralism of the architectural Indian landscape often quoted by Charles Correa [2].

Indigenous Technologies and Self-Costruction
–

Despite the assumptions quoted above about climate and a non unitarian colonialist condition of India, some techniques and construction solutions occur in the form of 'recurrences' which persist, indifferent to language and historical periods. Time is innerly handled in different ways of 'self-construction' that blend construction practices consolidated with innovative technologies that could be called 'indigenous'. 'Indigenous technologies' assume in this context the importance of high and wide connection with the environment and the society, involving use and adaptation at places [3]. These technologies not only share building practices but also assume an anthropological meaning in the use made of it in everyday life. The first 'recurrence' is definitely the open circular space intended as a place of sharing, of recollection and neutral in relation to the multi-religious practices of India. This type of space can be near built spaces, or by its own, as the symbolic value is given by the form itself. Very often it is a place that allows the seat slightly underground (ex Cept Ahmedabad) or it is simply designed in such a way as to create recollection. This persistence is probably due to the need, in a context so lush and sometimes even violent as the tropical, to find, in some occasions, a more sure perimeter.

Another recurrence, typical of tropical environments, but here highlighted because often added to existing buildings, is the porch. Porch intended not only as a shaded place of transit, but often 'inhabited'. This tropical declination of the porch, that is losing its public characterization to move to a private one, represent a new way of living spaces

after the construction. Natural environment is definitely another 'permanence' and it's an element to be mentioned for its vigorous strenght, either invasive to the ground, with roots that often dominate buildings, either on facades where very often it invades the materials used on the surface. It 's a permanence that Indians take for granted but which in reality is a variable very strong and difficult to manage in the time transformations.

Shading are definitely the most common constructive solution for tropical climates, and India is not an exception. Indian shadins have some special features that make them typical, as for example, be very thick horizontally (designed for the sun from coming from south) and are part of the construction. Often they are not hanging in a later stage but very often they are part of the technical installation and the language of the building. Many of these types of shadings do not present solar performance or any particular solar path study, but are the result of the experience of the industry that widely uses building tradition and imitation to build. These small elements are of different sizes —often brick or brick and cement—well expressing the modernity merged with indigenous technologies we were speaking above.

Another type of shading is what we might call 'light shell', which instead is leaning outside the windows and often is fixed with self construction techniques. In this case the rule is viceversa to give a contribution to light distribution and interior comfort. The majority of these components do not have security features that are delegated to metal bars which are present also in height in buildings, related to issues of possible intrusion but also to poultry.

Finally the theme of ornament that here in India expresses the desire of appropriation of space with indigenous techniques. It has a value and meaning much higher than the western understanding of ornament, because it takes values linked to popular beliefs and to the slow use in time of space. Indian ornament theme is often shifted from the rich ambit of fabrics, with a lot of details, ancient symbols and delicate motives that come from more important architecture.

As Correa emphasized in different texts, in India 'the builder is the user' because of the tropical climate that makes outer space a place to conquer in relation to thermal, solar and sometimes human very difficult conditions.

The Future of the Fully-Developed Handicraft
–

The occurrences highlighted above well suit possible technical developments in order to design processes of advanced craftmanship, which could cover new methods of construction, related to the context but at the same time susceptible to different degrees of innovation [4]. The major innovations that can be introduced are methods of dry assembly, which well fits for tropical environments and places where adaptation to the context needs constant changes, hybridization of traditional materials with contemporary techniques, creating mixed solutions that accentuate the materiality of solutions enabling at the same time more technical performance or aesthetic results and finally the increase in durability to a climatic condition that can be very aggressive in both seasons.

The local economy has made of expertise relating to the transmission of knowledge that is likely, in time, risky of being lost due to a globalization of methods and processes often disrespectful of indigenous reality, economically very fragile.

On the other hand, it is possible to record an increase in university education that attracts many students, who are aware that the country's resources can be high thanks to a knowledge that does not necessarily flow from industrialized countries but is settled and conquered on the ground. The two elements combined, allow to glimpse a promising scenario to the creation of an advanced craftmanship linked to construction and able of answer to a social demand for cultural recognition without giving up to contribute to the advancement of the technology sector of architecture.

These prospects highlight thus a very large horizon of new skills, models of development of the built environment and more advanced interactions between civil society and changes on the internatio-

nal scenario, positioning India and its mutating context, among the countries that will certainly have to challenge a human democratic evolution, that long since, the country is pursuing.

[1]
B. Melotto, *Elogio della differenza*, Agathon, pp 67-69, no. 4, July 2013.

[2]
C. Correa, *The New Landscape*, The Book Society of India, Butterworth Architecture, NY, 1989.

[3]
G. Tillotson, *Paradigms of Indian Architecture: Space and Time in Representation and Design*, Routledge, 2014.

[4]
E. Sumida Huaman, Bharath Sriraman, *Indigenous Innovation: Universalities and Peculiarities*, Springer, 2016.

architects in the tropics

/

MAPS + TIMELINES BY GIACOMO ARDESIO

The architects who were involved in developing the protocol for modern cities and towns in India were the ones who had cultivated a new sensibility of modern planning and design. Each of them arrived in Chandigarh with a mature aesthetic vision of their own, but in the many years they spent in India they had to learn a different way of approaching and implementing projects of architecture. It was on their later travels that this new awareness became the crux of a conscious and civilized way of respecting the environment, the resources and the energies of societies in which progressive changes were being made through architecture. From the perspective of this book a significant role was played by Otto Koenigsberger, who would continue to operate in both the East and Africa, laying the foundations of the development plans of what are now two of the world's mega cities: Lagos and Singapore.

OTTO KOENIGSBERGER
1908–1999
/

Legend:
— RESIDENCES
• ▪ ▫ ▲ CITIES
— TRAVELS

SELECTED PROJECTS

1939 Malleswaram School, Bangalore, India
1940 Shimoga College, Shimoga, India
1940 Engeneers' Association, Bangalore, India
1942 Broadcasting House, Mysore, India
1944-45 Victory Hall at Indian Institute of Science, Bangalore, India
1944-45 Master Plan, Jamshedpur, India
1946 Dining Hall at Indian Institute of Science, Bangalore, India
1948-51 Master Plan, Rajpura and Nilokheri, India
1948 Master Plan, Bhubaneswar, India
1949 Master Plan, Faridabad, India
1950 Master Plan, Chandigarh, India
1950-51 Master Plan, Gandhidam, India
1956 UN Housing mission in Accra, Ghana
1957 UN Housing mission in Pakistan
1959 UN Housing mission in the Philippines
1963 UN Housing mission in Singapore
1964 UN Housing mission in Zambia and Lagos
1966 UN Housing mission in Ceylon
1968 UN Housing mission in Brazil
1970 UN Housing mission in Penang
1978 UN Housing mission in the Philippines

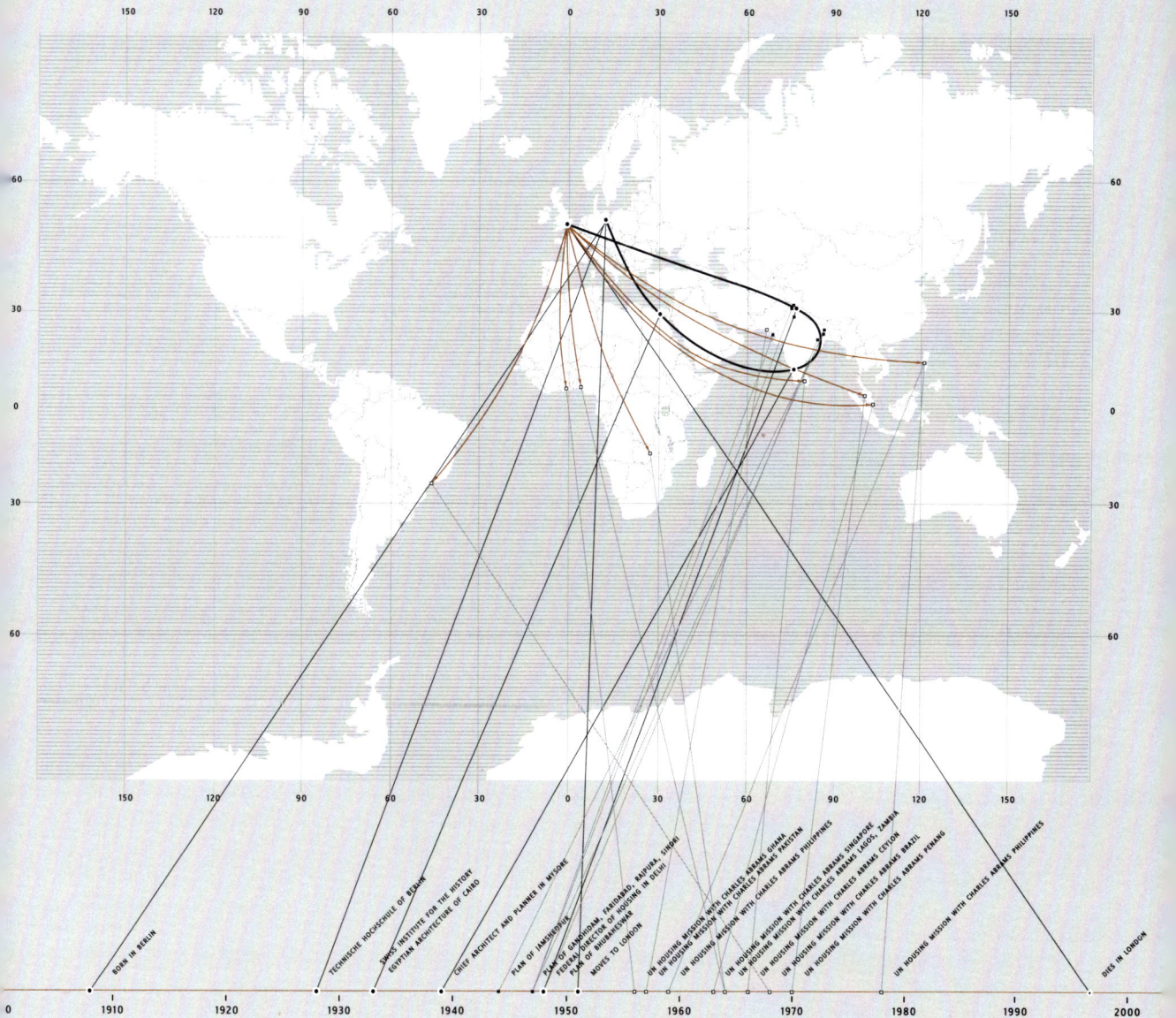

Timeline labels:
BORN IN BERLIN
TECHNISCHE HOCHSCHULE OF BERLIN
SWISS INSTITUTE FOR THE HISTORY
EGYPTIAN ARCHITECTURE OF CAIRO
CHIEF ARCHITECT AND PLANNER IN MYSORE
PLAN OF JAMSHEDPUR
PLAN OF GANDHIDAM, FARIDABAD, RAJPURA, SINDHI
FEDERAL DIRECTOR OF HOUSING IN DELHI
PLAN OF BHUBANESWAR
MOVES TO LONDON
UN HOUSING MISSION WITH CHARLES ABRAMS GHANA
UN HOUSING MISSION WITH CHARLES ABRAMS PAKISTAN
UN HOUSING MISSION WITH CHARLES ABRAMS PHILIPPINES
UN HOUSING MISSION WITH CHARLES ABRAMS SINGAPORE
UN HOUSING MISSION WITH CHARLES ABRAMS LAGOS, ZAMBIA
UN HOUSING MISSION WITH CHARLES ABRAMS CEYLON
UN HOUSING MISSION WITH CHARLES ABRAMS BRAZIL
UN HOUSING MISSION WITH CHARLES ABRAMS PENANG
UN HOUSING MISSION WITH CHARLES ABRAMS PHILIPPINES
DIES IN LONDON

Timeline years: 1910 1920 1930 1940 1950 1960 1970 1980 1990 2000

MAXWELL
FRY
1899–1987

/

SELECTED PROJECTS

1948 Mampong Teacher's
      Training College
      and Prempeh College,
      Kumasi, Ghana
1949-60 University College, Ibadan,
      Nigeria
1950 St. Francis College, Ho Hoe,
      Togoland
1950 Adisadel College
      and Wesley Girls' High
      School, Cape Coast, Ghana
1951 Adisadel College, Cape
      Coast, Ghana
1951-53 Housing, Chandigarh, India

1953 School at Mawuli, Ghana

1954 School and College,
      Aburi, Ghana
1956 Co-operative Bank, Ibadan,
      Nigeria
1958 Oriental Insurance
      Building, Calcutta, India
1959 Schools, Lagos, Nigeria
1960 BP office, Lagos, Nigeria

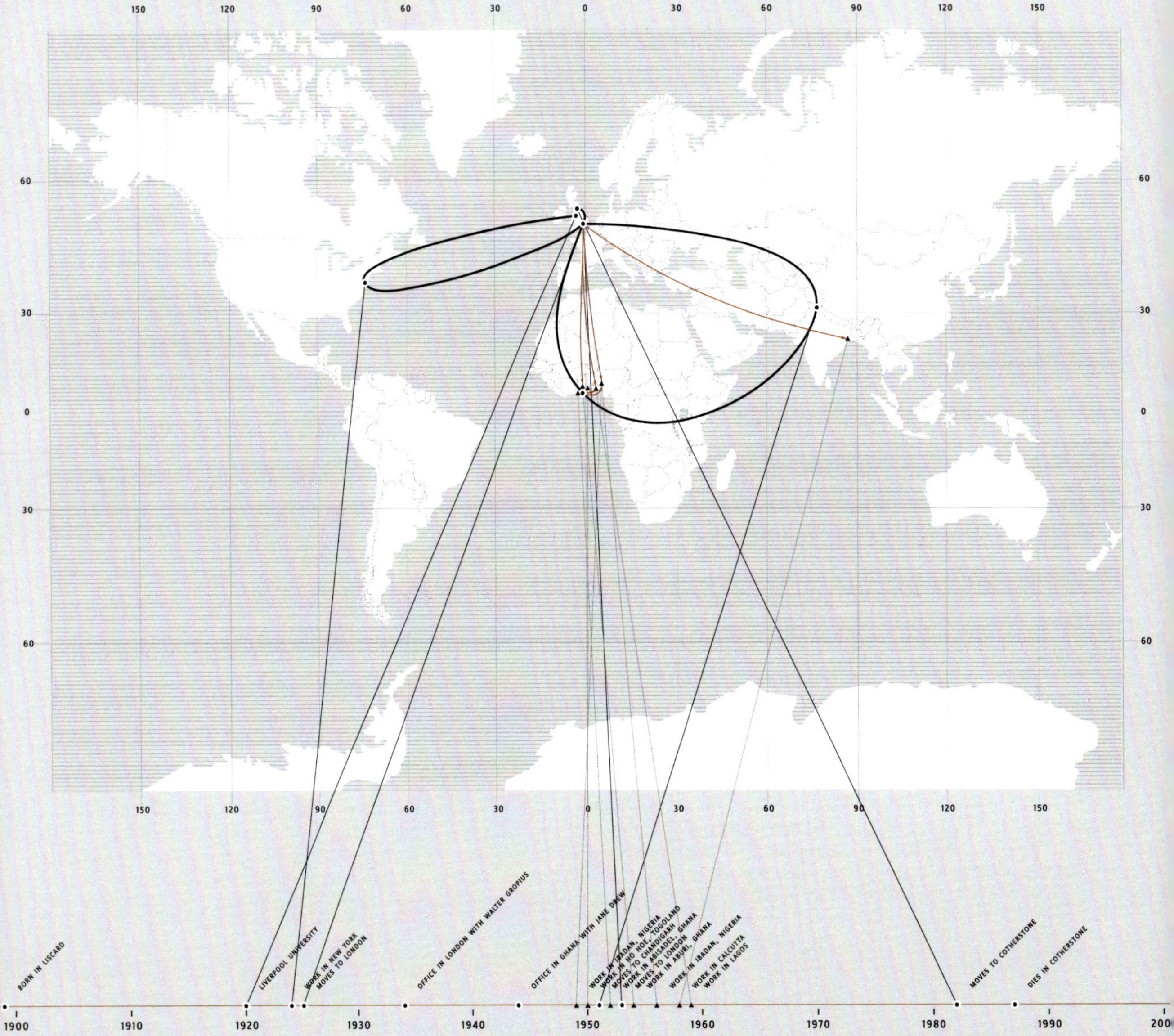

─────── RESIDENCES

• • ▪ ▫ ▲ CITIES

─────── TRAVELS

BORN IN LISCARD

LIVERPOOL UNIVERSITY

WORK IN NEW YORK
MOVES TO LONDON

OFFICE IN LONDON WITH WALTER GROPIUS

OFFICE IN GHANA WITH JANE DREW

WORK IN IBADAN, NIGERIA
WORK IN HO HOE, TOGOLLAND
MOVES TO CHANDIGARH
WORK IN BELSHELL
MOVES TO LONDON, GHANA
WORK IN LONDON, NIGERIA
WORK IN IBADAN, NIGERIA
WORK IN CALCUTTA
WORK IN LAGOS

MOVES TO COTHERSTONE

DIES IN COTHERSTONE

1900   1910   1920   1930   1940   1950   1960   1970   1980   1990   200

WARM MODERNITY

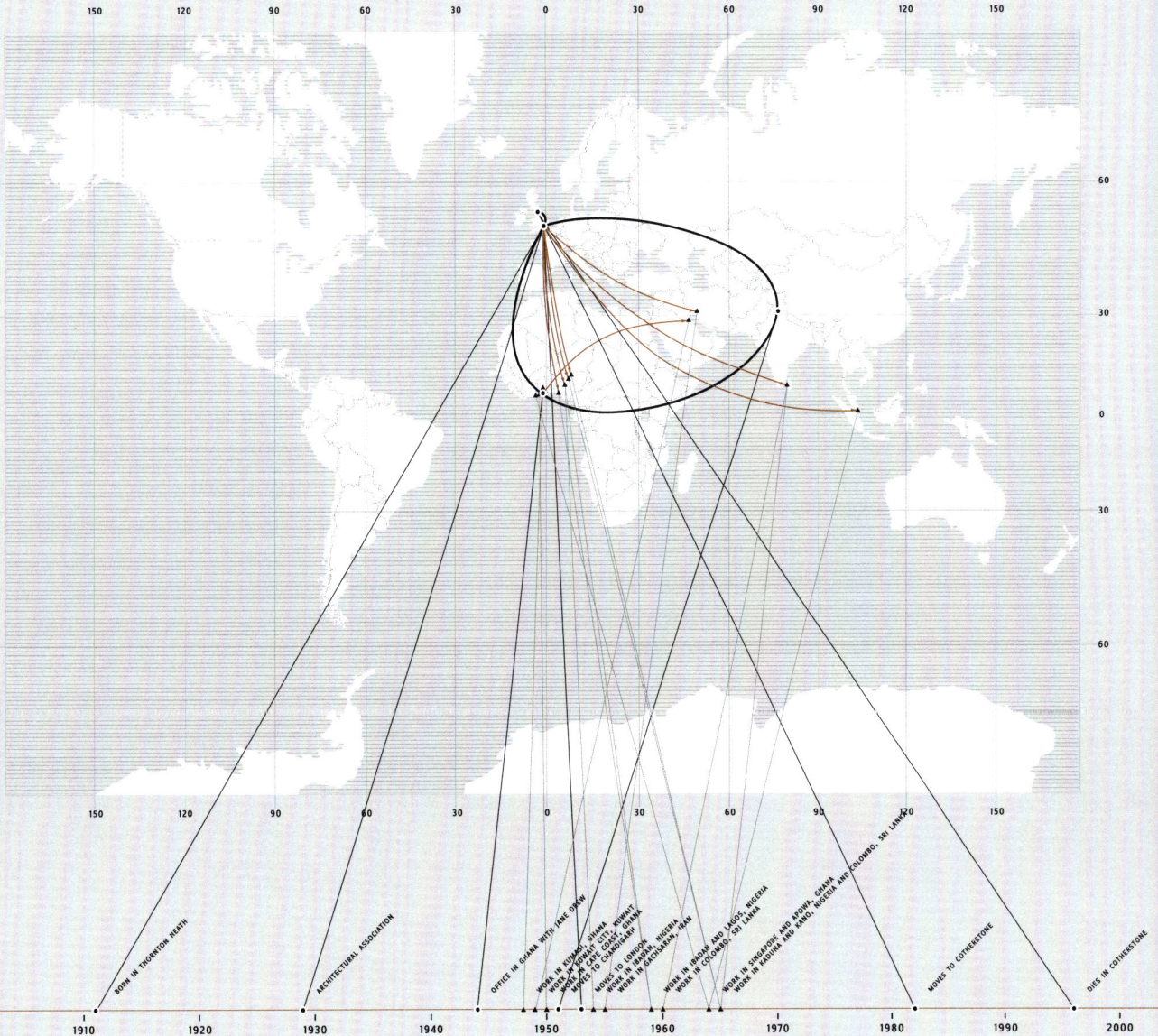

JANE DREW
1911–1996

/

RESIDENCES

CITIES

TRAVELS

SELECTED PROJECTS

1948   Teacher's Training College, Mapong, Ghana College, Kumasi, Ghana

1949   Hospital building for the Kuwait Oil Company, Kuwait City, Kuwait

1950   Adisadel College and Wesley Girls' High School, Cape Coast, Ghana

1951-53   Housing, Chandigarh, India

1953-59   University College, Cooperative Bank, and Assembly Hall

and Maisonettes, Ibadan, Nigeria

1955   Housing at Masjid-i-Suleiman, Gachsaran, South Iran

1959   Cooperative Bank, Lagos, Nigeria

1959   Cooperative Bank, Ibadan, Nigeria

1960   Lionel Wendt Art Memorial Centre, Colombo, Sri Lanka

1964   Training Centre, Apowa, Ghana

1964   Shell Headquarters in Singapore

1965   Ahmadu Bello Stadium

and Swimming Pool, Kaduna, Nigeria

1965   Women's' Teacher Training College, Kano, Nigeria

1965   Hotel in Colombo, Sri Lanka

BORN IN THORNTON HEATH

ARCHITECTURAL ASSOCIATION

OFFICE IN GHANA WITH JANE DREW

WORK IN KUMASI, GHANA

WORK IN KUWAIT CITY, KUWAIT

WORK IN CAPE COAST, GHANA

MOVES TO CHANDIGARH

MOVES TO LONDON

WORK IN IBADAN, NIGERIA

WORK IN GACHSARAN, IRAN

WORK IN IBADAN AND LAGOS, NIGERIA

WORK IN COLOMBO, SRI LANKA

WORK IN SINGAPORE AND APOWA, GHANA

WORK IN KADUNA AND KANO, NIGERIA AND COLOMBO, SRI LANKA

MOVES TO COTHERSTONE

DIES IN COTHERSTONE

1910   1920   1930   1940   1950   1960   1970   1980   1990   2000

Indian Architecture Building Democracy

LE CORBUSIER
1887–1965

/

RESIDENCES
CITIES
TRAVELS

SELECTED PROJECTS

1929 — Plan for Rio de Janeiro, Brazil

1932 — Plan Obus, Algiers, Algeria

1936 — Consultant for the Palace of Ministry of National Education and Public Health, Rio de Janeiro, Brazil

1949-53 — Curutchet House, La Plata, Argentina

1951 — Master Plan for Chandigarh, India

1951 — Mill Owners' Association Building, Ahmedabad, India

1951 — Villa Sarabhai, Ahmedabad, India

1951-56 — Villa Shodhan, Ahmedabad, India

1951-56 — Sanskar Kendra Museum, Ahmedabad, India

1952 — Palace of Justice, Chandigarh, India

1952-68 — Museum and Art Gallery, Chandigarh, India

1953 — Secretariat Building, Chandigarh, India

1955 — Palace of Assembly, Chandigarh, India

1956 — Baghdad Gymnasium, Baghdad, Iraq

1959 — Government College of Art (GCA) and the Chandigarh College of Architecture(CCA), Chandigarh, India

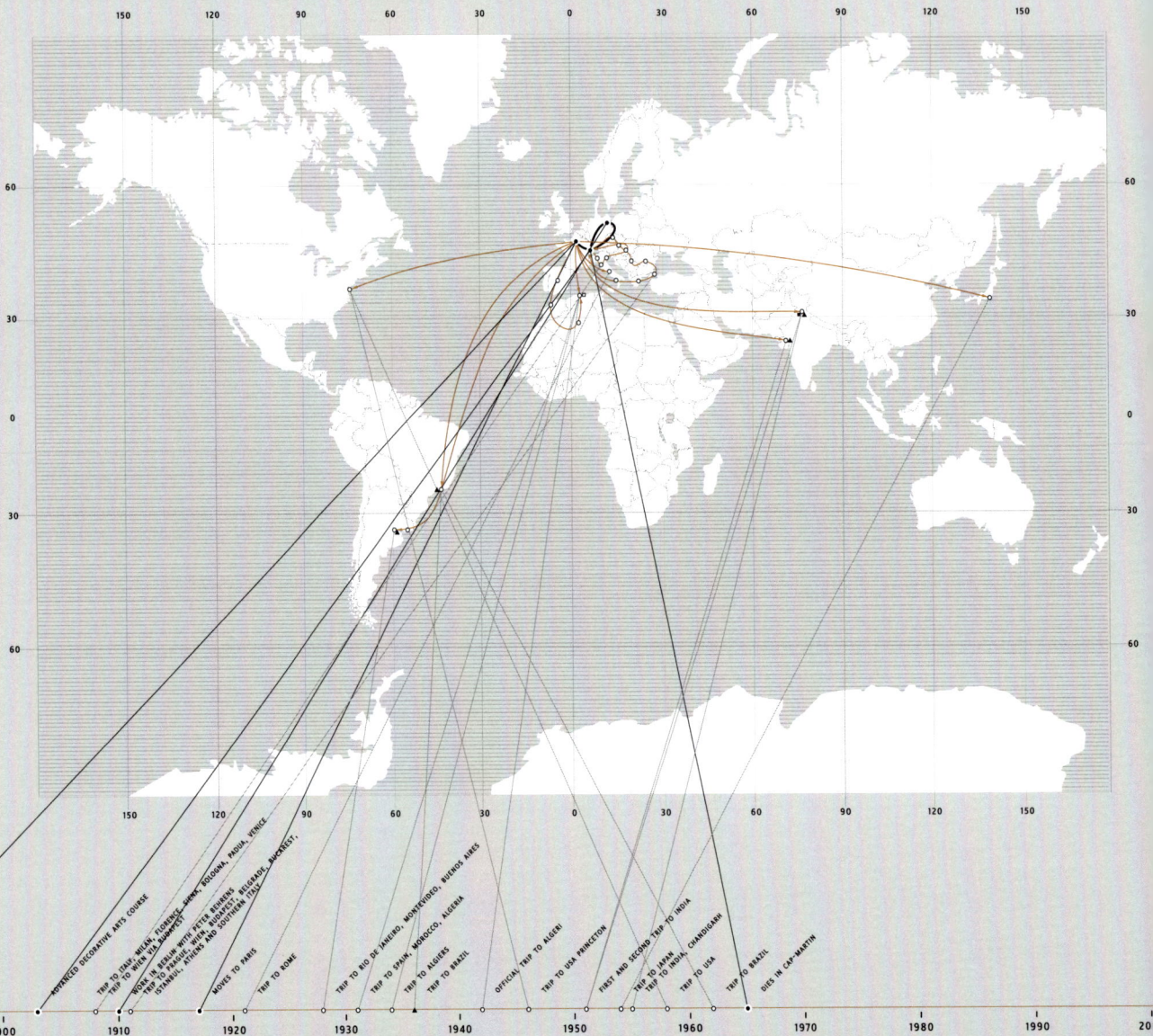

ADVANCED DECORATIVE ARTS COURSE
TRIP TO ITALY: MILAN, FLORENCE, SIENNA, BOLOGNA, PADUA, VENICE
TRIP TO WIEN VIA BUDAPEST
WORK IN BERLIN WITH PETER BEHRENS
TRIP TO PRAGUE, VIENNA, BUDAPEST, BELGRADE, BUCHAREST, ISTANBUL, ATHENS AND SOUTHERN ITALY
MOVES TO PARIS
TRIP TO ROME
TRIP TO RIO DE JANEIRO, MONTEVIDEO, BUENOS AIRES
TRIP TO SPAIN, MOROCCO, ALGERIA
TRIP TO ALGIERS
TRIP TO BRAZIL
OFFICIAL TRIP TO ALGERI
TRIP TO USA PRINCETON
FIRST AND SECOND TRIP TO INDIA
TRIP TO JAPAN
TRIP TO INDIA, CHANDIGARH
TRIP TO USA
TRIP TO BRAZIL
DIES IN CAP-MARTIN

1900 1910 1920 1930 1940 1950 1960 1970 1980 1990 20

WARM MODERNITY

ALBERT MAYER
1897–1981

/

SELECTED PROJECTS

1946 Master Plan, Kampur, India
1947 Uttar Pradesh Pilot Development Project after known as Etawah Project, India
1947 Consultant on the Master Plan for Greater Bombay, India
1949 Gujarat University Master Plan, Ahmedabad, India
1947-51 Master Plan for Chandigarh, India
1952 Uttar Pradesh General Community Development

1952 Project, India consultant to the Damodar Valley River Development Project, India
1957-71 Consultant on Master Plan for Ashdot, Israel
1957-71 Consultant on Master Plan for Delhi, India
1960 Consultant for Bangkok Masterplan, Thailand

—— RESIDENCES
• ▪ ◻ ▲ CITIES
—— TRAVELS

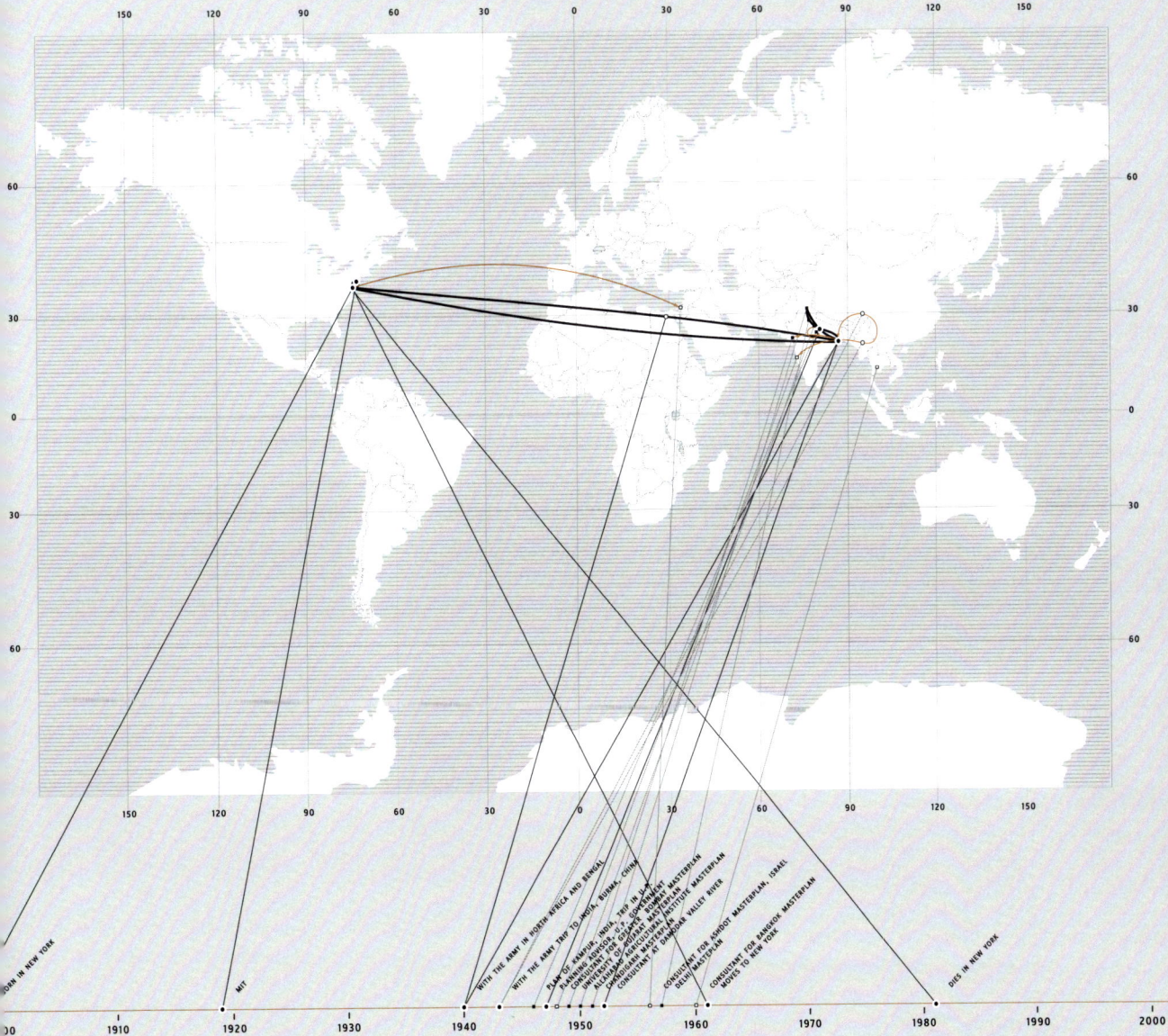

BORN IN NEW YORK

MIT

WITH THE ARMY IN NORTH-AFRICA AND BENGAL
WITH THE ARMY TRIP TO INDIA, BURMA, CHINA
PLAN OF KAMPUR, INDIA, TRIP IN UP
PLANNING ADVISOR - U.P. GOVERNMENT
CONSULTANT FOR GREATER BOMBAY MASTERPLAN
UNIVERSITY OF GUJARAT MASTERPLAN
ALLAHABAD AGRICULTURAL INSTITUTE MASTERPLAN
CHANDIGARH MASTERPLAN
CONSULTANT AT DAMODAR VALLEY RIVER
DELHI MASTERPLAN
CONSULTANT FOR ASHDOT MASTERPLAN, ISRAEL
CONSULTANT FOR BANGKOK MASTERPLAN
MOVES TO NEW YORK

DIES IN NEW YORK

1910   1920   1930   1940   1950   1960   1970   1980   1990   2000

OTTO KOENIGSBERGER

–
1908–1999

HE HAD SOUGHT REFUGE IN INDIA and was granted citizenship of the country, a status that he maintained for much of his life. He arrived there after a short stay in Egypt to obtain a PhD in archeology. When called on to prepare a versatile protocol for the modern town that would be able to bring India into the modern era, he came up with the band town pattern: an urban paradigm that could be adapted to pre-modern contexts. To draw up the actual plans for the foundation of modern towns in India, he assembled teams of Western and Indian architects, creating the preconditions for specialist training through direct action.

At the end of his period in India he moved to London, where he set up the Department of Development and Tropical Studies at the Architectural Association along with Jane Drew. From there he traveled to Africa to give his advice on development in Ghana in 1956 and to draw up the plan for the urban area of Lagos in 1964.

On innumerable occasions he gave lectures and provided advice on bringing improvements to countries in the tropical belt, from South America to the Middle East. In 1989 he was awarded the UN-Habitat Scroll of Honor for lifetime achievement.

JANE DREW

–
1911–1996

ONE OF THE CHIEF PROMOTORS of the subsidiary of the CIAM called MARS (Modern Architectural ReSearch), she was for a long time Assistant Planning Adviser to the Resident Minister for the British West African Colonies. With her husband Maxwell Fry and Pierre Jeanneret she then spent three years at Chandigarh during its planning and construction.

Her work as an architect was focused chiefly on the design of homes suited to undeveloped local contexts, in which extended families would be able to make use of ample joint spaces and open-air yards, given the favorable conditions of the climate. She also promoted the design of schools and institutes of training and assistance at which it would be possible to experiment with new activities, including communal ones.

MAXWELL FRY

–
1899–1987

ALREADY ACTIVE in the International Federation for Housing and Planning (IFHP), he had an opportunity to study and try to understand social systems and ways of life based on ancient customs in the African villages of the Gulf of Guinea. He professed the need for specific expertise in order to operate in depressed situations bordering on endemic poverty. In his view it was necessary to find a mode of coexistence with environmental systems—the topography of the area, the prevailing winds, the water supply—and with local populations, so that the capacity to develop and construct lasting settlements depended, in the first place, on an understanding of the existing situations and a redefinition of the role of architecture.

LE CORBUSIER

–
1887–1965

HE HAD ALREADY MADE his second visit to North Africa and proposed his plan for Algiers (Plan Obus, 1930-1931), as well as two trips to Brazil in 1929 and 1936, when he had come into contact with Lúcio Costa and Niemeyer over the project for the Ministry of Health and Education.

Together with his cousin Pierre Jeanneret and his longtime collaborator Charlotte Perriand, he was persuaded by the engineer P.J. Varma to become involved in drawing up the master plan for Chandigarh. On his arrival he joined an experienced team that had already produced a first proposal for the plan of the city. His ability to frame the new guidelines for an architectural language of tropical modernity within a mature aesthetics led to the city becoming an international symbol of the new modern and democratic India.

ALBERT MAYER

–
1897–1981

AN AMERICAN ARCHITECT and city planning, he had already drawn up a housing policy (1937) for the United States government that was centered on the creation of neighborhood units and promoted the construction of housing on a large scale in the regions around Cleveland, Sant'Antonio and Miami. Summoned by Nehru in 1945, he was put in charge of pilot projects in the rural areas of Uttar Pradesh and later became Planning Advisor to the state government. In Chandigarh in 1949, together with Matthew Nowicki, he came up with the first version of the superblock: although based on the neighborhood units of the band town pattern, this allowed the residential areas and city to grow to a larger size. At his suggestion adaptable models of housing were developed that could be constructed rapidly using simple technology.

Rahul Mehrotra

Md'A — During the years of the Independence Nehru chose for India to introduce Modernity. What did it mean?

MEHROTRA — At the time of Independence, I think, what modernity meant for Nehru was really, genuinely, about constructing a national identity. We had conditions at that moment where India was an incredibly diverse landscape—diverse in terms of religion, diverse in terms of culture, diverse in terms of languages.

I think Nehru's project with modernity was twofold, one was thinking about connecting India to the world through the modernization process, the social modernization process and the physical modernization process, but I think it was also about creating a kind of mutual ground under which all this diversity could nestle itself. So it was a very ambitious project because it had many agendas. Along with industry, it had agendas of national identity construction, it had agendas through modernization in terms of society modernization; of trying to create new markets, new multiple (models of) industrialization, creating new forms of infrastructure, but basically creating a society that through the process of modernization could be cohesive because the growth in India was very unequal. In the sense that the urban areas had been exposed to global networks and to modernization, whereas the rural areas were medieval in some cases—whether it was the caste system, or its forms of infrastructure—this was the big difference between the vision of Nehru and of Gandhi.

Nehru's was a vision came out of his own background, of education, but of being a very urban person, whereas Gandhi had seen the poverty in the lives of the Indian villagers, which is where he began some of his movements. Although the movements used the urban centers really to become visible, but Gandhi had the rural landscape in mind which was about a completely different form of development. One was looking to the rural landscape, looking at problems within society, looking at decentralized modes of manufacturing and making textiles, the weavers, he was worried about the farmers, he saw that as the real economy of India. Whereas Nehru's vision was very urban-centric and he saw the vision of India as being one which had to invest in the world, it had to be one that constructed this new national identity and had to be one where modernization also meant industrialization and also meant new modes of infrastructure and using infrastructure in all these different forms, including social infrastructure and physical infrastructure, as a way that the national identity could be constructed.

So in contemporary India, this becomes a very complicated question because maybe sixty percent of India yet lives in its villages and I think we are hoping or rather trying, by the year 2030 to become fifty percent urban. It means that it might be about rural landscape but the aspirations are all urban, the technologies that permeated these places and today with the internet and globalization nothing is unconnected. So I think that in today's India there is, for me at least, there is a blur between what is urban and what is rural. So the farmer who is manually ploughing his field in rural Uttar Pradesh in a farm near a village is also, while he is ploughing manually his field, he is listening to FM radio or on his cellphone he is checking the internet. Is he urban or is he rural? I mean, it becomes fuzzy, a blur. And so things are much more complicated in today's world.

Md'A — Nehru and Gandhi had different ideas for the development of the Nation: on the one hand an industrial country, and on the other an agricultural development. What is your retroactive opinion on this debate?

MEHROTRA — I think India's future is a "rurban" future. It's a future which will create this blur between the rural and the urban. Even in our existing large cities when you see big squatter settlements and you see the informal city and all of that, it is like the villagers invaded the city and conversely when we see different modes of development when we drive around in our villages you feel the city has invaded the villages. And so this has become a kind of mutual condition where the rural landscape goes into the urban landscape and the urban landscape goes into the rural landscape, and this is "the blur" that I am talking about. And so to think in terms of a paradigm that is "rurban," which combines maybe some of the community aspirations of smaller places of rural areas but also have the amenities of urban areas in terms of sanitation, health, education. I think it can be a wonderful paradigm. And, you know, just going back to the idea of the Third World as Nehru had with Tito and others, had promoted it, as a third option to the world of the Communism and the world of the Capitalism, a kind of hybrid notion. I think we, as designers and planners, have to think of what this could be, what a Third World urbanism means, what a Third World built environment means. My sense is that it would be a kind of hybrid which is a sort of mutated form of the modernity Nehru was talking about and it's also a mutated form of the ideal Indian village that Gandhi was talking about, so it's kind of in-between, and I think that's what's interesting but that what's also very difficult because (of what) it means for us as designers. It's hard to have a clear vision because when you have these kinds of third spaces and when you have this kind of hybridity it's also a lot of unexpected conditions. And therefore I think of how it challenges us as designers. It's a completely different role in terms of how we facilitate this environment, it's not about very specific visions but it's about how much of infrastructure, ways that you can facilitate growth in, and therefore I think, thinking through infrastructure, both social and physical infrastructure, becomes, very key to any imagination, to the "new modern" in the Indian context.

A DIALOGUE WITH | RAHUL MEHROTRA

MdA — The dualism modernity-democracy, or at least modernity-popular participation has characterized the entire second half of the twentieth century. This meant in India to promote an involvement of the population into the processes of transformation. In your opinion, how has the building industry for architecture and the construction of new cities contributed to the democratization of the country?

MEHROTRA — I think it is a very interesting question that you asked about Democracy and Modernity and the democratization process which is also a modern kind of invention. It pre-assumes many things, it pre-assumes education, it pre-assumes a political system that's open.
But the interesting thing is that Democracy hasn't really produced a clear city. You know, our old cities that we even today look at, when you look at Shanghai or Dubai and that show this very clear image of high-rise buildings or what I call "the landscape of impatient capital", in the sense, there is a clarity, we might not agree with it, but it's not a Democracy these are Autocracies which facilitate one single way of looking at something so the people in-charge decide there is going to be a financial center and then you make the terrain without any friction for capital to come and manifest itself. In a democracy, it is about a negotiated condition so you always get a mess. So maybe L.A. is the city of Democracy, but it has no a clear image or maybe it has a clear image of a different kind. So Democracies don't produce these kinds of visions that we as architects often allude to or refer to, when we're looking at cities, when we're looking at clarity of thinking, and vision, and plan, and built form, etc. And this is a paradox in a sense because while the modernization process even in the way Nehru imagined it, was a clear vision, but it was in the very initial stages of India's independence. So you could argue

it was also autocratic because Nehru made all the decisions, it wasn't a negotiated set of decisions—he decided! So when you look at Jamshedpur, and you look at Bhubaneswar, and you look at the second and third generation of cities after Chandigarh you begin to get the mutations that are inevitable in a democracy because these are negotiated conditions. So they are some traces, they are some reminiscences of the Garden City idea, of the kind of footprint of Chandigarh, or of the idea of neighborhood unit, but these are abstract, they get translated into protocols which become policy, and there is a big gap between the physical imagination of these spaces and the protocols and processes that are put into place to enable them to happen, and so you get a mutation. So by the time you come to Bhubaneswar and Jamshedpur and all these places, I think those really become the landscapes of Democracy within this process of modernization in India.

Md'A — With modernity were imported design criteria, technical specifications for building and administrative procedures of financial management of the space for a participatory collectivity. Which aspects have been absorbed by Indian architecture and which ones have been rejected?

Mehrotra — In my view there is a big disjuncture between the imagination of urban forms and then the units of architecture that then go into them, because, I think, the imagination of the urban form came from paradigms that were developed in the industrializing West, and they were reactions to the industrial project of overcrowding, and pollution and all of that, which is altered in the Garden Cities. It resulted in other forms of lower density, it also came out of the ability for individual mobility which was happening as part of the industrialization. So those paradigms of urban thinking, urban form, together they were applied to India as part of the modernization process. So whether it was Chandigarh, whether it was Bhubaneswar, Jamshedpur, all the other towns later on, they were architects who were beginning to think for the developing world so to speak, and for the Third World about architecture differently, about looking at the tradition and getting inspired by, looking at passive forms cooling and ventilation, etc. Maxwell Fry, Jane Drew. The idea of tropicalism, that is responding to the tropics, where you have to have the breeze moving through the humid air to cool—so cross-ventilation became important, like insulation: very simple principles can be applied.

There is politics involved here too, which had to do with funding because in the post-Colonial period a lot of the colonies were funded by Western counterparts, as a process, to help them make a transition to the modernization process. And so with that funding I think architects were challenged to make the money very effective, so you could do low cost housing, passive cooling, the solutions were very sensible, common sensible, efficient and all of that. In my view, that was the real root of the discussion on sustainability and I think tropicalism is linked very much to the origins of the question of sustainability. But somewhere in the 70s and 80s what happened is the high-tech architects in the West begin to use high-technology and they begin to justify this indulgence through sustainability as a idea or rubric and the debate about sustainability gets hijacked by the hi-tech architects. So I think that's where it lands—but its roots are in the 60s and 70s and in tropicalism.

But there is always a disjuncture between the architectural imagination and the imagination of the city, these don't fit together because for passive cooling, and heating and all of that, you need different kind of densities, you need

different kind of agencies like in traditional habitats, because it's not only the unit but how the unit aggregates that the
efficiency of all these parameters become visible. And so I
think this was the real struggle and I think this is why in
people's imagination that form of architecture never became
the common kind of architecture because it actually failed.
So while you can draw a beautiful section of these houses
and have an arrow that shows the air that goes through it,
actually they were very hot places to live in, because all the
walls were exposed, because it was a big house sitting in a
garden, sometimes. And so, in terms of the urban form, the
unit and the urban form didn't match. That means that the
urban form didn't come out from the unit and that imagination and vice-versa, and so I think this is a big disjuncture.
And this is why when you go in a lot of these towns at one
level you find them as very pleasant places because they are
lower density and as not as crowded as most Indian towns
and cities and so there is a kind of romanticism, especially
among the middle class, that is associated with these places.
But if you analyze it very deeply the units were not very efficient, the mobility systems were not very efficient and these
become places for the middle and upper middle class they
are not places for the poor really, because density doesn't
exist and often the public transportation mobility doesn't
exist. I think a lot of what came out from the process of
modernization in terms of the urban imagination was very
much linked to the idea that the nation will also be very big
middle class because in the imagination of modernization,
the creation of the bourgeois, the creation of independent
capital markets, you know, those imaginations with society
from which that particular form of architecture came never really happened in India. The middle class only now is
beginning to form in India. In India you have the very rich

A DIALOGUE WITH | RAHUL MEHROTRA

and you have the very poor, and now you're beginning to have a growing middle class. So forty years ago when a lot of these places were planned, they were planned with the imagination they were being made for the middle class but the middle class never existed actually.

Md'A — India has been an incredible laboratory to define the standards of tropical architecture. As a result, the solutions defined in the New Towns Protocol have migrated all over the world through the foreign architects who took part to this moment. What is the credit that India today can redeem by the other countries because of these models that have become a worldwide reference for tropical architecture and planning?

Mehrotra — So I think you are absolutely right when you state that some of the questions or issues that we are describing also resonate with Latin America, maybe parts of Africa.

What happened in these places was, between 1950s and 1970s, the kind of post-Colonial period, there were a lot of new nation states that were formed and in a lot of these nation states there were very complex places with complex histories and most of these leaders used modernization and projects of modernism as a way of constructing their new national identities. But in most of these places what happened was that the aesthetic modernity came to these places before the social modernization process and that was very quick to implement because you could built new towns, you could have a lot of housing, but there was no middle class, the society was not at the same level of modernization. And so all these disjuncture, and this mismatch between the society that occupied these towns and cities and the form of these cities, is very visible in many countries.

MEHROTRA — What happened in modern cities is, there is a new caste system which comes from the hierarchy of economics, so people who are richer live in one area because the houses are bigger, poorer people living in one area. So the society then gets organized according to economic categorization and their level in the government, but it's all to do with economy which means it's a new relationship that forms and in those new relationships people sometimes don't necessarily share culture in the same way and so therefore there is a big mismatch of communities in different neighborhoods. In the traditional urban paradigm, the way people were organized was consistent with the social status, probably the economic status but also the cultural beliefs and the religious beliefs, but that is broken down completely. So the new forms of the use of public space is more secular which is very good but then it is not that intense perhaps as in the traditional paradigms because of this disjunction, and this is the one of many disjunctures that modernism, or modernity, or modernization created in India. And of course there are many good things about it because it broke many of these old paradigms which divided people etcetera but I don't think we have yet found what would be the right formation of public space for these places. My own view, this is a personal view, is I think in these new paradigms infrastructure actually becomes the new public space so whether is railway system in Mumbai, or it's metro in Delhi or in Kolkata or it's other forms of infrastructure like community centers or cultural centers

A DIALOGUE WITH | RAHUL MEHROTRA

or performing art centers or art centers, these become the new public spaces in secular handy formation. And the unfortunate thing was that in a lot of the modern towns that were made in India, like Chandigarh and others , there wasn't adequate cultural and social infrastructure put in. People were relying on big open spaces as the public spaces, sometimes some museums were put on one side of it, but not adequately. So I believe that, the attention that was paid in these modern new towns in India, on efficiency, that I think the sacrifice that was made or what wasn't paid enough attention, was the social infrastructure that could make this society work together.

You know, I think all the new towns that were built in India, the one thing that is common to them all is that they are very low density, so they can actually absorb much more. I think the challenge for my generation of designer and for the next generation of designers and planners and urbanists will be how do you actually den-sify these places whether is Lutyens' New Delhi, which is very low density, whether is Jamshedpur, Bhubaneswar, or Gandhinagar—and what are the forms of interventions we make in these place that actually make them a much richer fabric. And for me at least personally, the work you all are doing in trying to put this document on new towns toge-ther is very important to lay those parameters out because this is outside the imagination of most planners. I think one of the problems in India is that everyone focuses on the megacity and everyone who comes from outside India goes straight to Dharavi but, you know, this wonderful landscape of new towns, small towns in India, which is where the future of urbanism is going to be. And, what I was referring to as the "rurban", the rural and the urban, will play itself out in these towns more than it will be in the megacities because these are on the perimeter of rural and urban areas, they also have a particular density which allows these kind of combinations to occur and I think this is going to be a big project for the future. There is a lot of potential and it's very possible to act in these landscapes and intervene as these are far less contested than our mega cities.

Md'A — Which is, instead, the direct legacy of this experience of this architecture that you received?

MEHROTRA — I would say my generation is the third generation maybe. The generation of Doshi, Correa and Raj Rewal is the first generation of Indian Modernists, then there is a second generation which comprises many Delhi-based architects like Romi Khosla, AGK Menon, KT Ravindran, Gautam Bhatia. So this is a generation which was a very important generation because that was the first generation that begun to think critically about these questions. But they also were practicing in a time in India, where it was under a socialism and so it wasn't free a market, they did not build extensively. So I think their contribution, for my generation, was critical thinking about these issues but not necessarily through demonstrations in practice—this is a history that hasn't been written. It's an entire generation that hasn't been talked about—maybe in five or ten years, when that generation is their seventies and eighties, someone can actually do something about that moment because it was an important transitionary moment between the first and the third generation. And for my generation the burden of modernism was much less because we are not concerned with national identity construction that is not

A DIALOGUE WITH | RAHUL MEHROTRA

even what politicians want to do today. We're engaging more the question of the region, we engage much more in questions of the cities we work in, we engage with different kinds of problems on the ground, and so the issues are different. We are right now participating in the contemporary so it's very difficult to even articulate what those issues are and someone will in twenty years talk about our contribution—maybe?

Md'A — In your opinion how should be a way for a current Indian modernity?

MEHROTRA — These are issues I have written about in my book (*Architecture in India since 1990*)—I think that the contemporary condition of India as a Democracy with its diversity, is really what I call a landscape of pluralism and many things coexist in bizarre ways that you can't imagine. It's a coexistence of very rich and very poor, of very old and very new, of also a schizophrenic condition. And so, in a condition like this, we almost have to separate aesthetics from the discussion about modernity. In a sense, the aesthetics of modernity could also be a very ancient aesthetic—as we are seeing in India. And so, I think, we are going through a true modernization phase now in terms of societial modernization because society is very mobile. Many social divisions have begun to break down, there is a lot of economic mobility as well as mobility of demography within the country, people of South India living in North India, it's all getting very mixed, and each one of them have their own sensibility, their own beliefs, their own religions, and therefore represent what they see or what they want to in the built environment in completely different ways. That's why in India you see real schizophrenia, there is no clarity in terms of imagery because our building construction industry is not yet industrialized because with industrialization comes a kind of homogeneity as it happens in China, as it happens in the Middle East, where buildings begins to all look the same. Whereas in India, because the protocols and the processes also are very diverse and the modes of construction are very diverse, you see it all coexisting simultaneously so it's interesting that the process of modernization, you cannot map onto the process of the built environment and it's aesthetic very easily. They always operate in a kind of separate way. And I think this is what I tried to understand in the book. Today, as a practitioner in India, one has to accept the simultaneous validity of these different modes of doing things, they're simultaneously valid. The wonderful thing about India is that it will always resist the project to be remade in one image, it will always want to make itself in many images, it's like our gods, there are thousands of gods, every god has a different image. So there is something about the Indian culture that supports and in a completely crazy way perpetuates, this pluralism in expression and I think this is part of our DNA and for architecture this is a massive challenge because as an architect you get schizophrenic because you have different clients so you have different aspirations of how they want to express themselves. And maybe because it's a big country with over a billion people it makes it very hard. And this is what makes India different from China.

In China now you have a younger generation that is trying to be more regional, there are smaller projects that have been built which use local materials but otherwise the fifteen new cities in China and the old cities, they are all been remade in a similar kind of paradigm—so it's making it very homogeneous. I feel, I am sure once you know Chinese cities, you go to a particular city, it has its own identity but

A DIALOGUE WITH | RAHUL MEHROTRA

from the outside they all look the same and you don't know how to differentiate them. But in India I think that is never a problem.

Md'A — In the contemporary, what problems need to be addressed?

MEHROTRA — I think one of the problems, which is a challenge for pedagogy and for teaching, but is also a challenge for the profession, is how we can spend more time on the middle scale. We spend time on the small scale and we jump to the very big scale. I think there's going to be more thinking on the middle scale which is in-between, the bridge, and so what is happening currently in the profession is: we have a lot of people who are fixed on the object, and what one can do with the object of architecture and then we have a lot of people who are working at the territorial scale, regional, abstracting, looking at the entire country and looking at all these patterns of urbanization. But there is a middle scale, which is the scale between the object and the territorial scale, which is the scale of the neighborhood and the scale of ten neighborhoods. Somehow that becomes for most designers, the least interesting, because in many ways it's also the most difficult because that's where the most commitments are really needed and the negotiations also the most complex! When you work with the middle scale it's when you have to really deal with many communities and that becomes the true form of Democracy but it also becomes the messiest, it also is the scale where you have the least control on architecture, it's the least abstract, it's the most tangible, and it's the one that we try to more or less always avoid. I think that is part of the problem.

So that's why Patrick Geddes was important, he was the only one who was taking the old town and trying to go through it and try to connect it with the new town. But the rest was like an utopian imagination that was part of modernism. Modernity was also utopian, it was ideological, it was about creating the new Vision. So part of the moving away from the old it had to have its own identity for making a new society and that was too complicated to deal with and Patrick Geddes was the only one who felt that through 'conservative surgery' we could upgrade the old and then extend their lives and relevance. His approach was of the biologist, more organic.

In order to do that we have to play a different role, and we have to play the role of advocacy, community organizers, activists, and it's also a role that is linked often to failure or said another way ,the risk of failure is much more. So when you work at a small scale with one or two clients, you feel it's in your control and when we work at a territorial scale we are not accountable to anyone, but there we are more arrogant. I am not saying it's not important because we look at patterns of urbanization and we hope maybe some politician will listen to us, right? But when we go to the neighborhood scale you have to deal with twenty-five families, their conflicts and differences, you are an activist. Architecture gets the most compromised at the middle scale and the risk of failure is much more at the middle scale and so we tend to avoid that. There are many architects who work at that scale but I think for the profession to be effective, and for the profession, to gain a respect in society again, I think that middle scale is what we have to deal with.

A DIALOGUE WITH | RAHUL MEHROTRA

WARM MODERNITY

BIBLIO–
GRAPHY

BIBLIOGRAPHY

/

AA. VV., *Africa, Big Change, Big Chance* (Milan: Compositori, 2014).

AA. VV., *Celebrating Chandigarh, 50 Years of the Idea* (Ahmedabad: Mapin Publishing, 2002).

AA. VV., *Charles Correa. With an Essay by Kenneth Frampton* (London: Thames & Hudson, 1996).

B. Albrecht, *Conservare il Futuro. Il pensiero della sostenibilità in architettura* (Padua: Il Poligrafo, 2012).

A. Aravena and A. Iacobelli, *Elemental: Incremental Housing and Participatory Design Manual* (Ostfildern: Hatje Cantz, 2013) - www.elementalchile.cl

G. Ardesio, *A Swarming City. Patterns of Interference* (Segrate (MI): Maggioli Editore, 2014).

T. Avermaete, S. Karakayali, M. Von Osten, *Colonial Modern, Aesthetics of the Past, Rebellions for the Future* (London: Black Dog Publishing, 2009).

G. Bachelard, *La philosophie du non: Essai d'une philosophie du nouvel esprit scientifique* (Paris: Presses Universitaires de France, 1966).

L. Benevolo, *Le origini dell'urbanistica moderna* (Bari: Laterza, 1991).

M.V. Capitanucci, "Balkrishna Doshi, Aranya Low-Cost Housing, Indore, 1983-1986", *Abitare*, no. 463 (Milano: Abitare, 2006), pp. 108-109.

M. Chatterjee, "The Evolution of Contemporary Indian Architecture", in AA. VV, *Architecture in India* (Paris: Electa Moniteur 1985).

C. Correa, *Housing and Urbanization* (London: Thames & Hudson, 1999).

C. Correa, *The New Landscape*, The Book Society of India, Butterworth Architecture, NY, 1989.

W.J.R. Curtis and B. Doshi, "Il piano di Vidyadhar Nagar, la nuova Jaipur, di Balkrishna Doshi", *Casabella*, no. 558 (1989), pp. 42-57.

M. D'Alfonso, in "Construir com imàgines, construir - Building with Images, Building for Real", in D. de Seta, G. Pagano, *Vocabulario de Imàgenes-Images Alphabet* (Barcelona: Lampreave & Millàn, 2008).

M. D'Alfonso (ed.), Michele Nastasi, *La Città sospesa: L'Aquila dopo il terremoto* (Barcelona: Actar, 2015).

M. De Michelis, *Heinrich Tessenow 1876-1950* (Milan: Electa, 1991).
I. de Solà-Morales, *Decifrare L'Architettura* (Turin: Allemandi, 2001).

M. de Solà-Morales, "Another Modern Tradition", *Lotus International*, no. 64 (Milan: Electa, 1990), pp. 6-32.

DW. Dreysse, *May-Siedlungen. Architekturfuerer durch acht Siedlungen des Neue Frankfurt, 1923-1930* (Cologne: Walther Koenig, 1994).

J. Drew and M. Fry, with H.L. Ford, *Village Housing in the Tropics* (London: London Lund Humphries, 1947)

G. Ferrero, *Rieducazione alla Speranza* (Milan: Jaca Book, 1988).

J. Flint, "Planned Decolonization and its Failure in British Africa", *African Affairs*, no. 328 (1983).

M. Foucault, *Des Espaces Autres in Architecture, Mouvement, Continuité*, no. 5 (Paris: Le Moniteur, 1984).

P. Geddes, *Cities in Evolution* (London: Williams & Norgate, 1915).

B. Ghosh, "New Towns in India, una casetta, una mucca, un acro di terra", *Lotus International*, no. 34 (Milan: Electa, 1982).

H. Henket and H. Heynen, *Back from Utopia* (Rotterdam: 010 Publisher, 2002).

F. Irace, "Intervista allo storico dell'architettura William J.R. Curtis", *Abitare*, no. 463 (Milan: Abitare, 2006, pp. 96-101).

I. Jackson, J. Holland, *The Architecture of Edwin Maxwell Fry and Jane Drew* (Franham: Ashgate, 2014).

H-U. Kahn with J. Beinart and C. Correa (eds), *Le Corbusier: Chandigarh and the Modern City* (Ahmedabad: Mapin Publishing, 2009).

R. Kalhia, *Bhubaneswar: from a Temple Town to a Capital City* (Carbondale: Southern Illinois University press, 1994).

R. Khalia, "Modernism, Modernization and Post-Colonial India. A Reflective Essay", *Planning Perspective*, no. 21 (Mumbai: 2006).

R. Koshla, "Indian Rural Architecture", *Lotus International*, no. 34 (Milan: Electa, 1982).

O. Koenigsberger, "New Towns in India", *Town Planning Review*, no .23 (London: 1952).

O. Koenigsberger, T.G. Ingersol, A. Mayhew, S.V. Szokolay, *Manual of Tropical Housing and Building* (London: Longman, 1974).

K. Joshi, *Documenting Chandigarh. The Indian Architecture of Pierre Jeanneret / Edwin Maxwell Fry / Jane Beverly Drew:1* (Ahmedabad: Mapin Publishing, 1999).

H. Lefebvre, *Le Droit à la ville* (Paris: Anthropos, 1968).

R. Lee, "Constructing a Shared Vision: Otto Koenigsberger and Tata & Sons, Architecture Beyond Europe", http://dev.abejournal.eu/index.php?id=356.

D. Lu, *Third World Modernism, Architecture, Development and Identity* (London: Routledge, 2010).

J. Masao Kamita, *Vilanova Artigas* (São Paulo: Cosac Naify, 2000).

B. Melotto, "Elogio della differenza", *Agathon*, no. 4 (July 2013), pp. 67-69.

R. Mehrotra, *Architecture in India since 1990* (Mumbai: Pictor Publishing, 2011).

R. Mehrotra, "Introductory Essay: The Architecture of Pluralism – 'A century of Building in South Asia'", *World Architecture: A Critical Mosaic, 1900-2000*, vol. 8, South Asia (New York: Springer-Verlag Wien, 2000, pp. 17-31).

R. Mehrotra, *Mapping Mumbai* (Mumbai: Design Research Institut, 2006).

R. Mehrotra, *Negotiating the Static and Kinetic City, the Emergent Urbanism of Mumbai in Other Cities, Other World, Urban Imaginaries in a Globazing Age by Andreas Huyssen* (London: Duke University Press, 2008).

R.R. Mehrotra, A.J. Agarwal, S. Ganguly, *Nehru: Man among Men* (New Delhi: K.M. Mittal, 1990).

M. Mostafavi, with G. Doherty, *Ecological Urbanism* (Zurich: Lars Müller Publisher, 2010).

S. Narang, "Overcoming the Partition Trauma", *Oxford Monitor of Forced Migration*, vol. 4, no. 2 (Oxford: Oxford University Press 2014).

J. Nehru, *Indipendence and After: A Collection of More Important Speeches of Jawaharlal Nehru from September 1946 to May 1949* (Delhi: The Publication Division, Government of India, 1950).

C. Pawlowski, *Tony Garnier et les débuts de l'urbanisme fonctionnel en France* (Paris: Centre de recherche d'urbanisme, 1967).

C. Perriand, *Une vie de création* (Paris: Êditions Odile Jacob, 1998).

R. Rewal, *Architecture climatique* (Paris: Electa Moniteur, 1986).

R. Riboldazzi, *La costruzione della città moderna* (Milan: Jaca Book, 2010).

R. Riboldazzi, *Un'altra modernità. L'IFHTP e la cultura urbanistica tra le due guerre: 1929-1939* (Rome: Gangemi, 2009).

J.M. Richards, "India Today", *The Architectural Review*, vol. 150, no. 898 (London: The Architectural Review Press, 1971).

E. Said, *Orientalism* (New York: Vintage Books, 1978).

D.G. Shane, *Urban Design Since 1945: A Global Perspective* (New York: John Wiley & Sons, 2012).

R. Sharma, "The Search for Roots and Relevance", *Architecture in India*, by AA. VV., (Paris: Electa Moniteur 1985).

S. Spataro, *Needs. Architecture in Developing Countries* (Siracusa: Lettera Ventidue, 2011).

G. Zucconi, *La città contesa* (Milan: Jaca Book, 1989).

THESIS

V. Baweja, *A Pre-history of Green Architecture: Otto Koenigsberger and the Tropical Architecture, from Principaly Mysore to Post-colonial London*, Michigan, 2008 - PHD Thesis.

E. Fiscon, *New Towns. Bhubaneswar. Sfide di modernità in India*, Milan 2013/2014 - Bachelor Thesis.

A. Nurra, *L'urbanistica tropicale di Otto Koenigsberger. L'introduzione del moderno a Jamshedpur, India*, Milan 2011/2012, Bachelor Thesis.

MADDALENA D'ALFONSO (Milan, 1972) is an architect and indipendent researcher, with a focus on interdisciplinary theoretical and visual analysis of contemporary architecture, art and the urban landscape.

She has written essays and curated exhibitions in Italy, Portugal, Brazil, Switzerland and the United States. She has promoted research on the city and urban imagery for the Fundação Gulbenkian in Lisbon, the Fundação Iberê Camargo in Porto Alegre, the Fondazione de Chirico in Rome, the MIT Museum in Cambridge (MA), the Milan Triennale and Milan Polytechnic. She teaches at the Milan Polytechnic and lectures at various international universities.

/ TIMELINE RESEARCH /

BETWEEN 2008 AND 2009 - The beginning of the Research presented in this volume started with Michele Vianello and with the magazine *Lars - Cultura y Ciudad*, and was published as an essay on the number 05_ 2009 in Valencia, with the title 'New Towns in India' and a little Survey of Alessandro Cimmino. Thanks Carlos Perez, Daria de Seta, Mariella Gramaglia, Alessandra Capurro.

BETWEEN 2008 AND 2012 - The Research proceed as a personal Study for the accompaniment of the Michele Vianello's Thesis at IUAV oriented by Paola Viganò - *Gandhinagar, the territory of a new modernity* - and as a Professor for the Thesis by Anna Nurra - *Tropical Urbanism of Otto Koenigsberger* - at the Milan Polytechnic. Thanks to Isa Consonni and Eng. Molteni for the support of the research missions. The work was presented by me and Anna Nurra in the debates of the World Urban Forum 6 UN-Habitat held in Naples in 2012.

BETWEEN 2013 AND 2015 - The research was consolidated through the exhibition project for the 14th Biennale of Architecture in Venice *Indian Paradigm, a model for a new modernity* curated with Giacomo Ardesio and the orientation as a Professor of the Thesis of Elisa Fiscon at Milan Polytechnic - *Bhubaneswar challenges of modernity*. Thanks to the Venice Biennale and Rem Koolhaas, The Embassy of India in Rome and Rahul Mehrotra. We also thank Christian Costranzo, Paolo Brescia and OBR, Matias Echanove, Marco Introini, Rachel Lee, Rajeev Lukad, Ipsita Mahajan, Ingrid Paoletti, Bimal Patel, Rahul Srivastava, Piyush Rout.

BETWEEN APRIL AND MARCH 2015 - Marco Introini did a Photo Survey in the relevant places of the Research: Jamshedpur, Chandigarh, Bhubaneswar and Faridabad to highlight the proximity between the Landscape of Indian Modern Cities and the Landscape of those kind of cities in Europe and the West.

BETWEEN APRIL AND SEPTEMBER 2016 - *Warm Modernity, Indian Architecture Building Democracy* was presented at the XXI Triennale di Milano, Design After Design, between 1 April - 12 September 2016. The design project was made by Giacomo Gatto and Pierpaolo Tonin with Samuel Colle. Thanks to Laura Agnesi, Giorgio Basile, Chiara Bodini, Pamela Campaner, Andrea Cancellato, Marzia Ferrari, Alberto Meomartini, Rajshree Pathy, Roberta Sommariva.

PERSONAL THANKS TO - Benno Albrecht, Giacomo Ardesio, Gabriele Basilico, Anna Braghini, Giovanna Calvenzi, Elisa Cattaneo, Isa Consonni, Ernesto d'Alfonso, Balkrishna Vithaldas Doshi, Alberto Ferlenga, Marzia Ferrari, Mila Ghiringhelli, Eng. Molteni, Rahul Mehrotra, Stefano Mandato, A. G. Krishna Menon, Ingrid Paoletti, Michele Pizzi, Ipsita Mahajan, Manish Prabhat, Raj Rewal, David Grahame Shane, Giovanni Singarelli, Gary van Zante.

PATRONAGE | **IDF** INDIA DESIGN FORUM. | **@Arc**

SPONSOR | ISAGRO ASIA  | EXPOWALL

PARTNER | **UniFor**

PROMOTER | **VA** VENTO &ASSOCIATI

Silvana Editoriale

Direction
Dario Cimorelli

Art Director
Giacomo Merli

Editorial Coordinator
Sergio Di Stefano

Copy Editor
Clelia Palmese

Production Coordinator
Antonio Micelli

Editorial Assistant
Ondina Granato

Photo Editor
Alessandra Olivari, Silvia Sala

Press Office
Lidia Masolini, press@silvanaeditoriale.it

Silvana Editoriale S.p.A.
via dei Lavoratori, 78
20092 Cinisello Balsamo, Milano
tel. 02 453 951 01
fax 02 453 951 51
www.silvanaeditoriale.it

Reproductions, printing and binding
in Italy
Printed by Intergrafica s.r.l. - Azzano San Paolo (BG)
April 2016